CONTENTS

Introduction

Violence in the Family is the twenty-second volume in the series: **Issues For The Nineties**. The aim of this series is to offer up-to-date information about important issues in our world.

Violence in the Family looks at the causes of domestic violence and the search for solutions. The information comes from a wide variety of sources and includes:

Government reports and statistics
Newspaper reports and features
Magazine articles and surveys
Literature from lobby groups
and charitable organisations.

It is hoped that, as you read about the many aspects of the issues explored in this book, you will critically evaluate the information presented. It is important that you decide whether you are being presented with facts or opinions. Does the writer give a biased or an unbiased report? If an opinion is being expressed, do you agree with the writer?

Violence in the Family offers a useful starting point for those who need convenient access to information about the many issues involved. However, it is only a starting point. At the back of the book is a list of organisations which you may want to contact for further information.

*****

What is domestic violence?

Take any street – your street. A quiet, comfortable place where people go about their business and all seems right with the world. Who'd guess that behind those firmly closed doors it's possible that a female neighbour is being abused by her partner?

It may be you who's being abused – if so, you may not want to admit it to anyone. It may be humiliating, embarrassing, and a painful reminder to you that the relationship you've been in for years isn't so happy after all. Often it's easier just to put up with it.

But the domestic violence that you, a female friend, colleague, relative, or neighbour may be experiencing is so common in Britain:

- research estimates are that from one in four to one in ten are victims
- that no one should feel a social outcast because of it.

Just what is 'domestic violence'?

The odd slap? An abusive threat? Sex when you don't want it?... Or a life-threatening attack? It is in fact all of these. Domestic violence is persistent and intentional abuse of any kind, whether physical, sexual or mental. In nine cases out of ten, the violence is inflicted by a man – often a husband or partner, but it can also come from a son, father, ex-husband or other family member. (source: Violence Research Unit, University of Wales, College of Cardiff) And don't dismiss violence handed out by a supposed friend. An incident in which you feel threatened by someone you know, even if it's miles from home, can also be classified as domestic violence. It happens everywhere, from large cities to rural communities, and to all kinds of women, from the wealthiest to the poorest, both able-bodied and women with disabilities. And don't think that beating a woman is necessarily an uncontrolled outburst – it needn't be. Sometimes it's a directed, purposeful act; the man knows exactly what he's doing. Of course, men feel a whole range of different emotions. A man might say he felt a surge of anger and couldn't control himself – you need to decide what you make of his words.

The media has recently highlighted the plight of 'battered husbands'; and violence can also occur in gay and lesbian relationships. But the majority of cases are where a man abuses a woman within a relationship.

You are not alone*

In the last year:

- As many as 1 in 10 women were victims of domestic violence
- 1 in 17 women were forced to have sex with their partners without consent
- 1 in 5 men struck their partners
- 6 in 10 men saw violence against their partner as an option.

Case history

Phyllida who is 28 and from Lowestoft, endured eight years of physical and sexual abuse.

'The violence started five days after we were married. It sounds a cliché but he literally changed overnight. It began when he threw a hot iron at me. I walked out after a week of it, but he always found me and brought me back. Once I spoke back to him after he beat me. He filled the bath with cold water and ice cubes and held my head under until I could hardly breathe. He let me up for air, then did it over and over again for an hour. I thought I was going to drown. Another time he put a rope around my neck and nearly strangled me. He performed marital rape time after time. I was hardly ever allowed out. He was a perfectionist and made me stay home and scrub the house from top to bottom. If there was one weed in the garden he would rub my face in it. He would take a ruler out and make sure the hedge I had trimmed was straight. He would pull out the cooker and fridge every week and I would

have to scrub behind them. And every day he would tell me I was useless, ugly, stupid. After a while I started to believe him. The only time I could go out was to the local shops. It was a 15-minute walk and when I got home he would examine me to see if I'd had sex with anyone. It was ridiculous. He had this philosophy that a woman is like a piece of meat – the more you beat her, the better she gets. By our first anniversary I had no feelings left for him. For the next seven years I just silently cleaned the house, or sat in the corner like a zombie. I finally escaped when he was asleep one night. I've been in a refuge four weeks now, and I'm starting to feel like a normal person again.'

Fact

Did you know that the phrase 'rule of thumb' is thought to have its origins in English Common Law? Even a hundred years ago, husbands were legally within their rights to physically chastise their wives, as long as they didn't use a stick any thicker than their thumb.

Demolishing the myths

Here are some popular misconceptions about domestic violence:

Myth: *It can't be that bad or the woman would leave.*
Fact: You may endure years of violence for a variety of important reasons: wanting to provide a home with two parents until the children have grown up; not having enough money to support yourself; fear of reprisal; worries about being stigmatised socially; fear of losing your home; and you may still love your partner.

Myth: *It only happens in working-class families.*
Fact: Any woman can be abused, no matter how much money you or your family have. Women who use refuges often have less access to money or other places to go. Some women contact Women's Aid for support and legal information rather than for refuge. There isn't one type of man who abuses – they come from every profession and every class.

Myth: *It's just the odd domestic tiff.*
Fact: Most of the time domestic violence happens on a regular basis; and can be anything from an abusive threat to rape or murder. Mental abuse can include being locked away in a cupboard or deprived of food and sleep.

Myth: *Only men who drink or have chauvinistic attitudes hit their wives.*
Fact: Domestic violence can't be blamed on alcohol. Drink may trigger violence, but it can also provide an easy excuse. It may be more comforting for you to believe that your partner wouldn't have hit you had he been sober.

The above is an extract from '*When home is where the hurt is*' produced by BBC Radio Two Social Action Team.

* From *The Hidden Figures: Domestic Violence in North London*, Middlesex University Centre for Criminology.
© *BBC Radio Two*

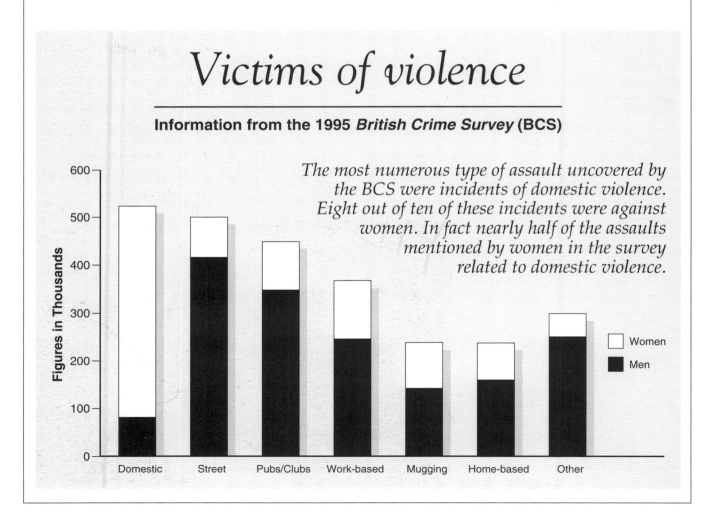

Victims of violence

Information from the 1995 *British Crime Survey* (BCS)

The most numerous type of assault uncovered by the BCS were incidents of domestic violence. Eight out of ten of these incidents were against women. In fact nearly half of the assaults mentioned by women in the survey related to domestic violence.

The extent of the problem

Few people realise that **domestic** violence accounts for a large part of the nation's crime.

The following statistics give an indication of the extent of this crime. Bear in mind that, due to considerable under-reporting, these figures are likely to underestimate the actual level of domestic violence.

Crimes of domestic violence committed by men on women account for a very large part of personal violence:

- 45% of female homicide victims were killed by present or former partners compared to 8% of male victims. (Criminal Statistics 1992, Home Office).
- Several small sample surveys have suggested that one in four women will have experienced at least one act of violence by a partner at some time in their lives (Andrews, 1987; Painter, 1991; Mooney, 1993).
- Domestic violence offences comprise around 25% of all assaults recorded by the police (*British Crime Survey* [BCS], 1989 Jones et al, 1986, Dobash and Dobash, 1980). The BCS further showed that, if only the most serious assaults were considered, over a quarter of these were also domestic violence.
- The Home Office Violent Crime Survey 1989 suggests that domestic violence offences comprise between 10 and 15% of all offences of violence against the person offences recorded to the police.
- Incidents of domestic violence were the most numerous type of assaults uncovered by the BCS, 1992 (estimated at 530,000 in 1991).
- Eight out of ten incidents were against women and nearly half of the assaults mentioned by women were of this type (BCS, 1992).
- In 90% of incidents of domestic violence, children are in the same room or the next room (Hughes, 1992).
- In 68% of incidents of violence against the mother, a child witnesses the assault (Leighton, 1989).
- A third of children present during an incident of domestic violence intervened to try to protect their mother (Hammer, 1990)
- Only around one-fifth of all incidents of domestic violence are reported to the police (BCS, 1992).
- In 1993 there was a 24% increase in reported domestic violence in London (Shirley Tulloch, Metropolitan Police).
- Domestic violence is as common an occurrence for women aged 16-29 as is pub-related violence for men in the same age group (BCS, 1992).
- 90-95% of domestic violence victims in the home are female (also true in Canada and the USA). In Western Europe, 20-25% of women will experience domestic violence in their lifetime – 10% in any one year (Dobash, 1994).
- In HM Prison Styal, 55% of the population of 200 women had been the victims of sexual abuse as children, or other forms of violence largely in a domestic context (George Walker, Styal).
- Around one-third of all divorces result from violence by husbands against wives (Parker, 1985).
- 40% of abused women have difficulty sleeping, 46% felt depressed and lost confidence (Mooney, 1993).
- 80% of abused women seek medical help at least once and 40% sought it on a minimum of five separate occasions (Dobash and Dobash, 1984)
- One-third of social work cases involve domestic violence (Maynard, 1985).
- In 1993 17,000 households were accepted for permanent re-housing by local authorities in England where the reason given for the loss of the last settled home was the breakdown of a relationship with a violent partner.
- Every year Women's Aid England provides help and refuge for around 30,000 women and children escaping domestic violence; a further 100,000 are given help and support.

'Domestic' was defined for the BCS as an assault when the assailant was a partner, ex-partner, household member or relative, or when the offence occurred in the victim's home or in the home of a friend or relative.

© Home Office News Release 24th October, 1994

Abused women

Myths and reality

Domestic violence – the mental, physical and/or sexual abuse of women by men they are, or have been, in a relationship with – is surrounded by myths and prejudices. Most of these blame the woman, for being abused, for staying with the abuser. At best, they are unhelpful. At worst, they put women's and children's lives at risk. These myths are common throughout society, in the media, in the police, sheriffs and judges, in doctors and nurses, in teachers, social workers, housing workers, in workplaces, in families. So women who are being abused, who are considering what their options are and trying to decide what they want to do, are confronted at nearly every turn by these myths and prejudices. This article contrasts reality with some of the most commonly held myths. But there is one point which overrides all the others – women are never to blame for being abused. The use of violence, verbal abuse, sexual abuse, is a choice men make to exercise power and control over their partners.

Myth: *She must deserve it or provoke it.*

Reality: There is no justification for using violence, unless your life is in danger. No-one deserves to be abused, and there is always an alternative, no matter how angry you are.

Myth: *She must enjoy it, otherwise she'd leave.*

Reality: Women stay with abusive men for many reasons, but not because they enjoy being abused. They may not know they are entitled to permanent re-housing if they leave home because of violence, and think they would be homeless. They may not know they are entitled to Income Support for themselves and their children, and think they would be penniless. They may fear they would

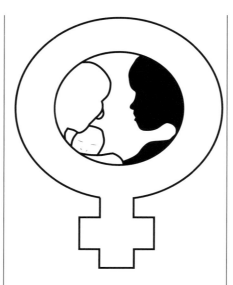

SCOTTISH WOMEN'S AID

lose their children if they 'desert' their partners. They may not know Women's Aid can provide safe, secret refuge, and fear that they would be found wherever they tried to go. They may feel that it is unfair to take the children away from their father. They may feel the abuse is their fault, and that they do not deserve a life free from violence. Or they may have been told by their partner that he will find them and kill them if they try to leave. None of these has anything to do with enjoying being abused.

Myth: *It's just the odd domestic tiff. Everybody has arguments.*

Reality: The difference between the occasional argument, which all couples have, and domestic violence is that the latter is quite deliberate behaviour which is used by men to exert power and control over their women partners. A range of different types of controlling behaviours are used, from depriving her of money or sleep, criticising her appearance, telling her who she can be friendly with, locking her in the house, hitting her, pulling her hair, hitting her with

weapons, raping her, threatening to kill her and her children.

Myth: *It's all caused by drink.*

Reality: Some men only abuse their partners when they have been drinking, but some only do it when they are sober, and some do it drunk or sober. Drink can provide an easy excuse, but is more of a trigger than a root cause of violence.

Myth: *It only happens in problem families.*

Reality: Men from all walks of life, all ethnic backgrounds and all ages abuse their women partners. There is no typical abuser, and no typical abused woman. Women's Aid has helped women whose partners were doctors, social workers, ministers, solicitors, psychiatrists. Most of the women who come to Women's Aid for help have no problems in their lives other than those caused by their partner's violence. Once they have escaped from the abuse, most women are as capable of leading a normal life as anyone.

Myth: *These men must be mentally ill.*

Reality: For a lot of people, it is easier to believe that an abusive man is mentally ill than it is to accept that he knows exactly what he is doing when he assaults, or rapes or tortures his partner. Most men who abuse their partners are only violent to them, never to anyone else. Most men who abuse are able to function normally in society, in the workplace, in all their other contacts with people.

Myth: *Men who abuse were abused themselves as children.*

Reality: There is no evidence that there is a 'cycle of violence', whereby children who were abused, or who witnessed abuse, go on to become abusers themselves. Many men who abuse come from families with no history of violence. Many have brothers who are not abusive. Children who witness abuse do not automatically grow up to be violent towards their partners, many completely reject the use of abusive behaviour as a result of their experiences.

Myth: *It was a one-off. He's really sorry, and it won't happen again.*

Reality: Once a man has started to abuse his partner, it is likely to happen again. It is rarely an isolated incident, usually it is part of a pattern of controlling behaviour, which may not have been recognised as such, e.g. telling her what to wear, who to see, being very possessive and jealous. Men often say they are sorry afterwards, making promises never to do it again. Often women who have left return to violent partners because of these promises, and there may be a 'honeymoon' period when he appears to be the perfect partner. However, most abusers will abuse again, maybe in a different form, and women should be wary of their promises.

Myth: *Women should stay for the sake of the children. Children need a father.*

Reality: Children who experience domestic violence suffer emotionally and some may also be physically or sexually abused. Many women leave when they see the effects on their children of their partner's abuse. Children's emotional and physical health tends to improve when they come into refuges. Children need love and security, which they can get from their mother, more than they need a 'father figure', especially one whom they know to be abusive to their mother. Some children of abused women do, however, have a good relationship with their father, and want to continue to see him. Access visits can be arranged to allow this to happen. Women and children have a right to a life free from violence, for the sake of both the women and the children.

© *Scottish Women's Aid*

If you are an abused woman...

You are not the only one
Studies suggest that one woman in four is physically assaulted by her partner. Domestic violence cuts across all classes, religions and ethnic groups.

You are not to blame
Men who abuse their partners are responsible for their own behaviour. Your partner will have learned to use violence as a way of dealing with his feelings of anger and frustration long before he met you. Violence is not their only choice in reacting to domestic problems.

Assaulting a woman is a criminal offence
Woman abuse represents 25% of all recorded violent crime.

You cannot change your partner's behaviour
The only way for the violence to stop is for your partner to recognise that he has a problem and to seek help for his behaviour.

You do not have to put up with it
It is against the law for a man to assault his partner. The police can arrest him and lay charges. You can see a solicitor about getting an injunction, which is a court order telling your partner not to molest, assault or harass you and your children.

Ignoring a beating can be dangerous
Even the first attack should be taken seriously. Studies show that violence escalates over time. What starts off as an occasional shove may, in some cases, turn into violent and regular beatings.

Seek legal advice
From a lawyer who considers woman assault a crime. A women's refuge or the Law Society can provide you with a list of solicitors. You might be entitled to Legal Aid. You may also be eligible for preliminary advice and assistance under the 'green form scheme'. The Citizens' Advice Bureau has lists of solicitors who carry out Legal Aid work.

Contact Refuge or your nearest refuge
Refuges can give you support and practical information (income support benefits, housing rights, schooling, etc) as well as emergency accommodation. You do not have to be physically abused to obtain help from a refuge. They also help some women who are emotionally and sexually abused. Many refuges provide telephone counselling .

Do not keep the assault a secret
You have nothing to be ashamed of. There are people who can and will help you. Do seek help. Your GP or hospital casualty department can record your injuries. Your doctor may be an important witness in court. If your helper is unsympathetic, look for help elsewhere.

Break your isolation
The more isolated you are, the greater your dependence on your partner. Isolation and dependency can make it difficult for you to take constructive action. Increase contact with others, get help. Remember. You do not have to put up with abuse. No one is entitled to control you or to use violence to get their way. In an emergency, contact the police or a Woman's Refuge.

© *Refuge, 1994*

'So why don't they leave?'

There are a combination of reasons why women don't leave, or return time and again to violent relationships. The practical alternatives for women wanting to escape violence and live without fear are still limited by many factors that are outside their control.

- Homelessness
- Isolation and loneliness
- Childcare responsibility
- Economic dependency
- Appalling levels of state benefits
- Immigration laws

Inarguably, Asian women are more vulnerable and isolated generally; and by the very nature of their situation, those experiencing violence in their homes will also face considerable constraints. Although domestic violence is now widely held as unacceptable in the Asian community, there are many cultural and social pressures that continue to tyrannise Asian women into staying in violent relationships, or returning to violent partners. The fear of reprisal is a major consideration for all women seeking to escape. For Asian women the urgency and immediacy of this fear can only really be appreciated in the context of the community backlash, which has encouraged and sanctioned the unlawful activities of 'bounty hunters' and other vigilante-style guardians of Asian women's *izzat*. The woman is still believed to uphold not only her own honour, but also that of the assailant, the family, and the wider community.

The shame and stigma of separation or divorce still has a powerful hold on Asian women's lives. Women fear that they will be condemned by the religion-wallahs or the self-appointed spokesmen of their communities. They are persuaded to stay for the 'sake of the children',

> **46% of women who suffer violence do not report the crime for fear of reprisals, and many do not think they will be believed or taken seriously**

especially the girls, for 'who would marry her if she left her husband?'. So they wait for their children to grow up, wait for their husband to change; submit to pressure from family and friends to reconcile with him, time and again. Not withstanding the emergence of more Asian women's refuges and active voices from the Asian women's movement in Britain, the reality of living alone is neither appealing nor easy. Will they ever marry again, or find a caring relationship with a man who would accept their 'tainted' past? As one of our clients bluntly asks: how many men would readily marry a divorced woman with children, when they can go 'back home' and marry a pubescent virgin? The answer is: not many.

Furthermore the over-sensationalised issues of arranged marriages, dowry, run-away girls, and now the suicide rate, feed into prevalent racist stereotypes of Asian women as submissive, passive victims. Although these are important issues for Asian women, we object to these being used as a yardstick to measure the extent of our community's 'backwardness' and 'savagery'. These assumptions effectively act as a deterrent for many women wishing to leave violent relationships. If they approach a predominantly white agency or a mixed refuge, they are exposed to the possibility of further racism, either from individuals or through institutionalised racist practices that

neither recognise nor provide for different needs.

As Asian women providing a front-line service, the first and foremost consideration for Newham Asian Women's Project is to ensure individual confidentiality and safety by encouraging an atmosphere of mutual trust and respect. Our knowledge and insight into the specific socio-cultural pressures and needs that fundamentally differentiate the experiences of Asian women from other women mean that we are able to provide a specialist service.

Shantiben's story

Shantiben had suffered from domestic violence for most of her 30-year marriage. Her strict religious background prevented her from any thoughts of leaving her husband, as did the pressure from friends and family to 'make it work', even after her two children had grown up and left home. During one severe beating her husband threw her out. She came into our refuge feeling very afraid but also ashamed that she had left home. Once she saw that she was not alone, that there were other women in similar circumstances who did not judge her but helped and supported her, she began the process of rebuilding her life. Her children, happy that their mother had finally left home, were extremely supportive. She was eventually temporarily rehoused by the local authority, but has also been offered a self-contained flat in the Hamara Ghar project, where she will be living with other Asian elders and will not feel isolated. Shantiben has now settled into a happy and independent lifestyle.

The above is an extract from the Newham Asian Women's Project's Annual Report 1993/4.

© Newham Asian Women's Project

The legal options

Domestic violence – the legal process

The legal system is important in protecting the rights of people. In recent years great progress has been made regarding legislation designed to protect those suffering from domestic violence.

The framework of the law reflects the values of society. Using the courts can, however, be a daunting experience.

A helpful solicitor is a great asset. Women are likely to need a solicitor in connection with separation, custody, access to children, occupancy or disposal of the matrimonial home and division of other properties, plus obtaining Exclusion and Protection orders.

A solicitor's job is to act in the woman's best interests, drawing on expert knowledge to explain legal options.

It is important that the solicitor is understanding and supportive, as the legal process itself can be alienating to a woman. Women's Aid can recommend sympathetic solicitors who are experienced in matrimonial work.

Women's Aid can also support the woman through this process by outlining the sort of questions she will be asked, and preparing her to relate personal details about her relationship to the solicitor. We can also accompany her and sit in on the interview if required.

Legal Aid, i.e. help with costs, is usually available. Those solicitors on the Legal Aid list can be found at public libraries, Citizens' Advice Bureaux or local advice centres. After the solicitor is satisfied that proceedings can be taken, a court hearing will be arranged in about 1 to 2 months if it is to be heard in Petty Sessions as are Separation and maintenance orders.

Divorce and Wardship are heard in the High Court, wardship cases are likely to be heard sooner than this, if an emergency arises, while divorce may take longer. The time scale is likely to be longer in rural areas. If both parties are getting Legal Aid, no order for costs will be made – i.e. all will be paid out of the Legal Aid fund. If a wife makes a successful application to the court and her husband is not receiving Legal Aid, he may be ordered to pay costs. If a wife makes an unsuccessful application to the court, usually no costs are awarded against her.

Going to court

This can be quite an ordeal. Even the thought of going to court can produce a lot of anxiety, while the possibility of going into a witness box to give evidence can be quite intimidating for the majority of women. This is a time when Women's Aid can offer support. However, in many instances the man does not appear in court and the woman can proceed in his absence.

Matrimonial courts are private and confidential and not open to the press or public.

The law in this area is complex and decisions taken will have far-reaching consequences. The role of the solicitor is to advise on which of the following court orders are appropriate:

1 Personal Protection Order
This order forbids the man from assaulting or threatening the woman or her children.

2 Exclusion Order
This order excludes the man from entering premises where his wife is living (it may or may not be the matrimonial home) and prevents him from returning to it. The order can also be made to exclude the man from the surrounding geographical area.

If these orders are breached, they both carry the power of arrest, which means the police can arrest the man, detain him in custody and arrange for him to be before the court charged with breaking the order within 24 hours. However, the responsibility for bringing charges seems at present to rest with the woman. It is possible that the responsibility will be returned to the police by the introduction of new legislation or a reinterpretation under case law.

Emergency procedure

There is an emergency procedure available for both Protection and Exclusion Orders which means they should be obtainable within 24 hours. In rural areas there may be delays where the courts sit less frequently. Interim (emergency) Protection or Exclusion Orders can be granted without your partner being present in court. These emergency orders will last up to 5 weeks and can be renewed at a full hearing, if necessary. The Exclusion Order will last for a further six months. There is no statutory time limit for Personal Protection Orders but it is usual for them to be limited to a few years.

3 Separation
(Financial Provision Order)

When applying to the magistrates court for a 'separation', a woman is in effect asking for a judgement on maintenance to be paid to her, custody of the children, if any, and terms of access. If there is a dispute over custody the court will enlist the help of Social Services.

There are two ways to get a separation. The first is by agreement with both spouses, the second is by satisfying the court that one of the five grounds noted in the Domestic Proceedings NI order 1980 is present viz; that the other spouse has:

- failed to provide reasonable maintenance for the applicant.
- failed to provide reasonable maintenance for any child of the family.
- committed adultery.
- behaved in such a way that the applicant cannot be reasonably expected to live with him.
- deserted the applicant.

An application must be brought to the court within a year. If an order is granted, a variation can be made by either party if there is a change of circumstances.

Should there be a reconciliation for a period of six months or more, this order becomes invalid.

The above orders will all be heard in the Magistrates Court (Petty Sessions).

Deed of separation

A woman can get a solicitor to draw up a deed of separation. The deed could include the usual maintenance, custody and access details and possibly the man's agreement not to molest the woman. It may be turned into a court order and enforced by the Magistrate's Court if need be. Legal Aid is available.

4 Wardship

Wardship Proceedings should not be undertaken lightly, but it is sometimes in the interests of both mother

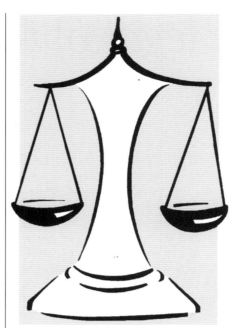

and children to do so. A woman can make her children 'Wards of Court' if, for instance, she fears the possibility of her children being abducted and taken out of the country. Wardship gives the woman legal protection against this and gives the court guardianship of the children. Wardship proceedings always involve Social Services and may mean them having a long-term involvement. However, the wardship will usually involve an amicable partnership with a social worker whose aim will be to have the order discharged sooner rather than later.

These proceedings are held in the High Court.

5 Divorce

It may be thought that the most obvious remedy for an abused married woman is to get a divorce. Yet factors keeping women in violent relationships also militate against applying for a divorce: there is no guarantee that violence will cease, and some women fear that court proceedings will only stir up violence again. Others do not consider divorce because of religious or cultural beliefs.

A woman can only apply for a civil divorce if her marriage is recognised as valid by UK law, if she has been married for at least two years, and if she or her partner is domiciled here, or if one of them has been resident here throughout the year before divorce proceedings begin.

She will have to prove that the marriage has irretrievably broken down for one of the following reasons: adultery, unreasonable behaviour, desertion for at least 2 years, separation for 2 years if the man agrees to a divorce, 5 years if the man objects.

If the woman anticipates any disputes over the divorce itself, the children or ancillary matters to do with property or money, she should consult a solicitor. Even in undefended cases it is best to get a solicitor's advice first.

The woman may be eligible for Legal Aid to get preliminary advice, to prepare petition documents and related applications, and for defended divorces.

6 Judicial Separation

Women sometimes opt for this order as opposed to divorce for religious reasons. The same grounds apply as in a divorce application and in all respects the same orders may be applied for. Financial settlements can be resolved but the marriage is not dissolved; therefore the parties are not free to remarry.

7 Redress for physical assault

The police are now committed to a 'new and more robust' policy, geared towards arrest and prosecution of perpetrators of domestic violence. This is to be welcomed, and will mean an increase in the numbers of cases brought to court. Women's Aid is fully committed to this policy, as we believe it will have a deterrent effect. However, recognition must be made that individual women will need a lot of support as a consequence. We are committed to provide this support, and would urge other agencies to do so in order that the policies will be effective.

8 Criminal injuries compensation

This may be a possibility where women have sustained serious injury. The assault would have to be reported to the police and medical evidence would be required. A solicitor experienced in this area should be consulted.

The above is from an information leaflet produced by Northern Ireland Women's Aid.

© Northern Ireland Women's
Aid Federation
June 1995

Different kinds of abuse

Mental cruelty – domestic violence without the bruises

You may have read this far and thought: 'None of this applies to me. My husband has never hit me.' But domestic violence isn't always physical. It can be mental, too. Not the odd shouting match that all couples have, but a psychological battlefield in which the woman is the loser. Family law solicitors say mental abuse plays a major part in up to 50% of the divorces they handle (source: *Solicitors Family Law Association*), and it's believed to be so widespread in Britain that if it were a disease, doctors would call it an epidemic.

Case history

This is Marian's story, she is 42

'My husband appeared to be the perfect husband to everyone. He was charming, intelligent and highly successful. I was quite naive when we met and from early on in our marriage he felt he could teach me the ways of the world. What it really did was feed his ego.

He started belittling me at parties, being patronising about something I'd said. Or he'd hide things deliberately and then demand to know where I'd put them. He was so convincing that I started to question my own sanity. Then he started comparing me to other women and no changes I made, such as new clothes or a new hairstyle, were ever right.

All my self-confidence went out the window. His behaviour had a sort of drip-drip effect on me – lots of little incidents that ate away at my self-confidence as if he was slowly poisoning me. It took 12 years of marriage before I finally left. If he'd been a monster and had hit me, I think I would have left a lot sooner.

But what he did was so subtle it was hard to recognise – especially for me.'

What role does alcohol play?

In many people's minds alcohol and domestic violence have always gone hand in hand. But how accurate is this idea? Drink plays a part in many domestic violence cases reported to the police but many men are stone cold sober when they commit their crime. There are conflicting opinions about whether drink causes a man to be violent. A man might use drink as an excuse when he begs forgiveness the next day: 'I'm sorry darling. It was the drink. It won't happen again.' It can allow him to deny he is violent. But a review of research around the world into the links between drink and violence done by the University of Missouri in 1990 found aggressive behaviour more likely when alcohol was present.

Home and away

Women in rural areas face their own set of dilemmas as victims of violence. Isolation, poor public transport and everyone knowing each other's business are all common problems. There is an added dilemma for women on farms who, by leaving, may well compromise their children's chances of inheriting the family property.

Case history

Hazel is a 25 year-old mother from Scotland

'My partner and two children and I were living in a town when the council rehoused us to a tiny village. We hadn't been getting on, and moving out there made it worse. He'd be abusive and would hit me there was no one around to stop him. Living in the town, at least I'd had my parents nearby to help me. And I could be anonymous; not everyone knew who I was or the state of my relationship. Now he had me on his own he could do what he pleased. We had houses either side so I suppose they must have heard us rowing. I had to hide the bruises every time I went out, and I felt like everyone was whispering about me. I never got invited anywhere – everyone was shutting me out. I didn't have a car, I couldn't drive, and the bus only came once a day. I felt trapped.'

● The above is an extract from *When Home is Where the Hurt is* produced by the BBC Radio Two Social Action Team.

© *BBC Radio Two*

The fear of going home

The charity Refuge has launched a campaign to raise awareness of domestic violence. Cherie Booth QC, who has acted for battered women, explains the need for funds

People who visit cinemas over the next month or so may be surprised to see an advertisement, launched by me earlier this week, to raise awareness of domestic violence.

I recently agreed to become a trustee of Refuge, the charity behind the campaign, which shelters battered women and helps them to rebuild their lives. It was a decision which had its roots in 1977, at the start of my legal career, when I found myself sent to courts in and around London to represent women who were seeking injunctions to restrain their partners from abusing them.

Domestic violence represents 25 per cent of all recorded violent crime in Britain, yet it is a crime which our society often prefers to ignore. At 22, I had no idea of the terrible things that could go on in the privacy of the home. I have never forgotten what I learnt.

Often I would turn up at court to meet my client and see the bruising, the scars, the gaps where her teeth had been knocked out. Sometimes the women would be pregnant (a quarter of all battered women are assaulted during pregnancy). Often the violence had taken place in front of their children. Frightened women would tell me of partners who had raped or sexually abused them.

Sometimes, I was threatened by those men myself – and was grateful that I had the court staff to protect me. My clients had to face the prospect of living with the threat and reality of violence at home, where there would be no one to protect them.

I would meet men who would tell me that it was all untrue – only for them to be proved to be lying in the witness box. Others would agree that they had indeed abused their

> *To escape, you need shelter, a refuge where you can be safe and start to put your life together. I often saw my clients return to violent homes simply because they had nowhere else to go*

partners, saying: 'She was asking for it,' and adding: 'It was only a cuff around the ear.' Often, they did not even realise that what they were doing was wrong, as though it was their right to punish their partners.

At first, I could not understand why my clients put up with the abuse. Why didn't they walk out? Chatting to them outside the court, I soon realised that it was one thing for me to say 'You must get out of this situation' and quite another for the women to act on my advice.

One reason was a simple and practical one: if you are a mother with children and no money of your own, where do you go? If you are an older woman, who may have been financially dependent on your partner for years, how do you walk out?

To escape, you need shelter, a refuge where you can be safe and start to put your life together. I often saw my clients return to violent homes simply because they had nowhere else to go. Even with the protection of an injunction, they were vulnerable. (According to Home Office research, 18 per cent of all homicides in England and Wales are wives killed by their husbands.)

For these women, a place like Refuge is a lifeline – a chance to break out of the pattern of violence that has ruined their lives and the lives of their children.

The human cost is enormous. So is the financial burden on the state. Police are called to the same households time and time again. Abused women and children end up in casualty wards. Families break up; many are rehoused in bed and breakfast hotels. Traumatised children often fail at school; some will drift into becoming juvenile offenders.

More than 12,000 women have poured through Refuge's doors since it opened in Chiswick, west London, in 1971. Not only does Refuge serve as a haven, it also works to restore women's self-confidence, which has been sapped by the denigration they have experienced, both physically and mentally.

If the women are truly going to build new lives for themselves and their children, they need help and support to enable them to believe in themselves again. Refuge does this by providing support and skilled counselling to the women and their children. It also provides practical help with rehousing and with advice on benefits.

The need for its services is as great as ever. There are not enough beds available. Often women will ring Refuge's 24-hour nationwide helpline, only to discover there is nowhere for them to go.

Yet Refuge teeters on the brink of closure through lack of funding. If it is to do its job properly, it urgently needs more money. By supporting this campaign and by supporting Refuge, we can assist women to escape from the misery that the crime of abuse brings.

© The Telegraph Plc
London, 1995

Michael Howard announces new circular to combat domestic violence

The next step in the Government's campaign to tackle domestic violence was outlined today by Home Secretary Michael Howard.

Mr Howard announced proposals for a new circular to encourage local organisations to work together to co-ordinate their response to victims of domestic violence.

It is part of the Government's comprehensive response to ensure that the perpetrators of domestic violence are brought to justice, that victims receive the emotional and practical support they require, and that measures are taken to prevent the crime.

Speaking at a meeting of the Women's National Commission in London, Mr Howard said:

'The Government is anxious to ensure that domestic violence is tackled vigorously by the criminal justice system and others.

'We must not be blinkered to the fact that domestic violence not only causes damage to its immediate victims, but may also affect children within the relationship.

'There is no quick solution to prevent such crimes but through a combination of increased public awareness, a firm response to perpetrators from the criminal justice system and improved inter-agency arrangements for responding to victims' needs, real progress can be made in the prevention of domestic violence.'

In October the Ministerial Group on Domestic Violence launched the Government's domestic violence awareness campaign in England and Wales, with the clear

> **The Government is anxious to ensure that domestic violence is tackled vigorously by the criminal justice system and others**

message that *Domestic Violence Is A Crime – Don't Stand For It.*

The campaign is to be complemented by a leaflet, produced in a number of languages and targeted specifically at women who may be reluctant to report domestic violence because of their immigration status.

Its message will be clear: nobody, whatever their nationality or immigration status, should have to suffer violence or abuse of any kind.

Mr Howard also spoke of the importance of a stable and disciplined family background in preparing children for adulthood. He said:

'Teaching children the difference between right and wrong is a process which must begin in the home and continue throughout childhood.

'We must continue to teach the importance of accepting responsibility for our own actions and of considering how our actions affect others.'

Home Office press release
December, 1994

Age breakdown of victims of domestic violence

Those aged 16 to 29 were overwhelmingly the most frequent victims of domestic violence.

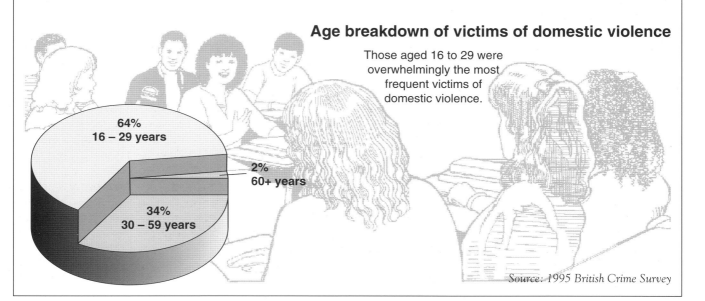

64%
16 – 29 years

2%
60+ years

34%
30 – 59 years

Source: 1995 British Crime Survey

Government's campaign offers victims little help

Government denies women the power to refuse domestic violence

The government's Domestic Violence Awareness campaign, launched today, claims to 'provide a source of help and advice' to victims of this crime. In fact it offers little or nothing in the way of services, protection, policing or resources. Many of the resources and agencies, to which women are encouraged to turn for help, have suffered massive cuts.

Unlike the local authorities' Zero Tolerance campaign, which also claims to raise awareness of domestic violence, this campaign denies the government's responsibility for women suffering violent crime in the family.

It is a response to a growing movement of women against domestic violence and against the outrageous neglect of victims by the police and services – reflected, for instance, in the film 'Ladybird, Ladybird'. Yet it claims to 'reduce costs' by avoiding 'duplication of effort'. Except for refuges, which are provided not by the government but by women themselves, there are no services specifically for women suffering violence. There is nothing to 'duplicate', and any 'cost-reduction' must mean cutting the police, the courts and the welfare state.

● While campaign literature encourages women to report to the police, all the Home Office can offer is that 'An initial telephone survey of all forces revealed many examples of good practice'! Women cannot count on either protection or law enforcement. Despite publicity, many women still tell Women Against Rape Britain (WAR) of a dismissive response, or of being held responsible for violence against them. Protecting women is still not a police priority.

● WAR's Ask Any Woman survey found that four out of five women unable to escape rape in marriage were trapped by lack of money and/or housing.

● One in five single mothers give violence as a reason for leaving a relationship. Government attacks on single mothers at home as 'welfare scroungers' deny mothers' right to financial independence from violent men and to recognition for the work they do bringing up their children.

These are some of the 'key agencies' the Home Office lists where women can go for help:

● Council Housing – this has shrunk. Mothers who leave violent men must wait months or years for housing.

● Refuges – provision remains grotesquely underfunded, with only a fifth of the places required for women and children. An extra £10,000 for Women's Aid's national helpline to 'assist' with increased demand during the campaign is an insult to the women who will be trying to get help. Where are they to go?

● Benefits – the Child Support Act, which forces women back into financial dependence on men, promotes domestic violence and has in at least one case led to murder. The campaign refers women fleeing violence to the social fund – but even payments for basic needs, like beds and cookers, 'can never be guaranteed' and, if agreed, are usually loans. Women disabled by violence face preposterous tests for the new Incapacity Benefit.

● Crown Prosecution Service – WAR is helping several women fight CPS refusal to prosecute rapists and batterers.

● Legal Aid for injunctions – cut. Many women on low wages cannot afford an injunction against a violent ex-partner.

● CABs – gone or disappearing from many high streets.

● Social services – legal responsibility to women facing domestic violence, and fewer resources for everyone. Despite the leaflet's assurance that 'In most cases this will not happen', victims of domestic vio-

lence are still having their children taken away by social services.

● Health – the leaflet for women states, with unbearable arrogance and sexism, that 'Many women don't realise the impact their partner's behaviour can have on their health.'

● Immigration – the Home Office enforces a policy of deporting women whose immigration status depends on their marriage to a violent man.

● Racism – the document recognises that Black women 'can face particular difficulties in getting appropriate support and advice, as they may face the dual problems of violence and racism'. It proposes no course of action.

● Compensation for victims of violence is not mentioned: Parliament confirmed the cuts in this Criminal Injuries resource a mere four days ago.

The campaign leaflet's emphasis on women's need to 'recognise' what's happening is a slap in the face for the thousands who have sought help and been denied it – and are then blamed for being 'confused', defeated or apathetic. The way to encourage women to seek help is to make that help available.

WAR London's forthcoming book *The Power to Refuse* will include a documented critique of how domestic violence is dealt with by police, courts and other state agencies.

Violence against women

From the Women's National Commission (WNC)

In 1992 45 per cent of female homicide victims were killed by their partners, compared to 8 per cent of male homicide victims. Fifteen per cent of all violent offences were classed as incidents of domestic violence in 1989 (compared with 10 per cent in 1985). [source: *Criminal Statistics for England and Wales 1991/ 92*]. In 1992 the number of domestic assaults reported to the British Crime Survey interviewers (this survey measured people's experience of crime in 1991) had risen by 79 per cent since 1981.

Violence against women, and the fear of such violence, curtails women's freedom and violates women's human rights. It is also a major deterrent to their full participation in society. We need strong preventative measures and sanctions against it.

The law on provocation works to the detriment of women because they often react in different ways to men.

Women who have been victims of violence need support in overcoming its physical and psychological effects. The WNC therefore welcomes action taken by the police to increase the number of 'rape suites', to train police officers in dealing with the victims of domestic violence, to increase the number of women police officers, and to develop victim support schemes.

Violence against women, and the fear of such violence, violates women's human rights

The voluntary sector too is playing an important part in developing support services for women who have been subjected to violence or the threat of it.

The provision of refuges for women suffering from domestic violence is very patchy across the country. There are only 280 refuges nationwide with very poor provision in rural areas.

The WNC welcomes the adoption by some local authorities (e.g. Edinburgh and some London boroughs) of the Zero Tolerance campaign which aims to make domestic violence socially unacceptable.

Recommendations

The government should legislate to change the definition of 'provocation' to include domestic violence for cause of provocation and delete the word 'sudden' from such definition.

There should be more information available to women on their rights and the improvement in police response. Government should extend the special Domestic Violence units to all police stations and support the setting up of a nation network of Rape Crisis Centres staffed by women.

Problems related to domestic violence should be taken more seriously by police and social workers, possibly thereby preventing some deaths.

There should be a nationwide network of refuges so that all women who need them have access to one.

We urge all local authorities to adopt the Zero Tolerance campaign.

● The above is an extract from *In Search of Equality, Development and Peace*, a report by the WNC in the context of the 4th UN World Convention for Women, Beijing, 1995.

The hidden victims

Children and domestic violence

Introduction

'*People think children are stupid you know, like dumb animals, but they know exactly what is going on. It isn't getting much out of a childhood. I went without a childhood.*' (child brought up in a household with domestic violence)

Professionals and the public have recently become more aware of the impact of physical and sexual abuse on children. Despite this, little is known of the effect that living in a violent household can have.

The Hidden Victims – Children and Domestic Violence reports findings from the first study carried out in Britain on the devastating effects of domestic violence on children.

Domestic violence is the second most common type of violent crime in Britain (over 25% of reported violent crime)[1]. In London alone, there were 9,800 domestic violence assaults recorded in 1992[2]. It is suggested that only 2% of such offences are ever reported.[3]

The research was undertaken because our family centres were concerned that domestic violence affected the lives of many mothers and children. Carried out in 1994, the research aimed to address our lack of knowledge about the impact on children, and increase our understanding of the type of help and support they and their mothers need.

Anonymous questionnaires were placed in NCH Action For Children's family centres across Britain. NCH Action For Children family centres are community-based resources which work with families and children experiencing a range of problems.

108 women, who had 246 children living with them, completed questionnaires. Further in-depth interviews were carried out with mothers and children.

Posed by model

Photo: NCH Action for Children

Summary of key findings

The violence experienced by mothers and children

A picture emerges of mothers, often with young children, suffering regular and systematic violence at the hands of their partners. The average length of the relationships was just over 7 years.

Most, 86%, said they had been slapped or punched, 63% strangled, 61% had been kicked, and 61% also said that they had been struck with an object.

'*He kicked me in the stomach when I was pregnant for him, I was about eight weeks and I suffered a threatened miscarriage… I didn't lose (my son) but it was close.*'
(MOTHER)

Many of the women, 83%, had experienced bruises or black eyes, 50% had been cut, 23% had broken bones and 40% had been to hospital for their injuries – 12% had been admitted for at least an overnight stay.

'*Every week I had one or two black eyes – guaranteed.*'
(MOTHER)

Almost half of the women (46%) said that they had been forced to have sex by their violent partner, 23% had been 'raped with threats', and 18% 'raped with violence'.

'*I love my son dearly, I adore him, but he was conceived in rape.*'
(MOTHER)

Two-thirds (69%) of women were regularly imprisoned in their home, actually or with threats, 65% prevented from speaking to other people, and 22% had their clothes taken away.

'*We were kept like prisoners, not allowed out, sometimes all weekend. We weren't allowed to see friends or to have friends back. He used to physically drag the children back in the house.*'
(MOTHER)

Children's experiences of violence

● Of violent men in the study, 83% were fathers to one or more children in the family.

'*He smashed my head against the wall because the baby was making a mess, and he picked up the dish and*

threw it at me and I was covered in baby food. I just collapsed on the floor. The baby was trying to pull me across the floor, crying "Mummy, get up".'
(MOTHER)

● 73% of mothers in the survey said their children had witnessed violent incidents, and 67% had seen their mothers beaten.

'My earliest memory was about the age of six . . . .I'd walk in and my mother would have a bloody nose or whatever and she'd be crying all the time …she told me it was an accident.'
(CHILD)

● 27% said their violent partners had also physically assaulted their children. Several said their partners had sexually abused their children.

'He used to hit me as well as my Mum … One time he smashed my head against the wall giving me a black eye, and I had to make excuses at school.'
(CHILD)

● 10% of the mothers were sexually abused in front of their children.

'I was raped once in front of the children, with a knife at my throat. The children tried to pull him off and it was awful.'

● 99% of the mothers said their children had seen them crying and upset because of the violence.

The short-term effects of domestic violence on children

Living in a violent home can impact on every aspect of a child's life and behaviour. In the short term, children may be fearful, withdrawn, anxious, aggressive, and confused, and suffer from disturbed sleep, difficulties at school and problems in making friends.

'My sister does stupid stuff, like she lights a match and burns her hand with it. And she's got scars on her arms.'
(CHILD)

● 91% of mothers surveyed believed their children were affected in the short term.

'My daughter was a bundle of nerves. She'd only have to see the car and

she'd be screaming in the street, "let's hide in here Mum"… she was glued to me.'
(MOTHER)

'I wouldn't eat for weeks on end. I lost a lot of weight, but I wasn't anorexic really because I would eat at school. I just wouldn't eat at home.'
(CHILD)

● 25% said their children had become aggressive towards them and towards other children.

'I was angry with my father . . . And I took it out on my mother as well, because she was still with him. I'd take it out on my brother as well . . .there was no loving any more.'
(CHILD)

● 31% developed problems at school.

'From the age of eleven I truanted. I couldn't concentrate on my studies, I couldn't focus.'
(CHILD)

● 72% said their children had been frightened, 48% that they had become withdrawn and 34% said they had developed bed-wetting problems.

'I just felt really insecure myself, because I don't know whether one day my Mum's not going to be there and he's going to turn round and have a go at me.'
(CHILD)

● 13% of mothers said their children had run away from home because of the violence.
● 31% said their children had intervened to protect them. 27% said their children had tried to protect siblings.
● 84% had found their children harder to look after in a violent situation because they were depressed; more than half thought this was because they were frightened or exhausted.

The longer-term effects of domestic violence on children

Many young people have vivid recollections of domestic violence. Longer-term effects include lack of self-confidence and social skills, violent behaviour, depression and difficulties in forming relationships. Disrupted schooling means children

fail to reach their potential while others leave home early to escape the violence.

'They remember the black eyes, the beatings, fighting and arguing, they remember it all.'
(MOTHER)

● 86% of mothers believed their children were affected in the longer term.

'You come close to breaking point. I felt suicidal a lot of the time, but I never carried it through, thank God now, looking back.'
(CHILD)

● 33% thought their children had become violent and aggressive and harder to control, 29% that they were resentful and embittered, and 21% that their children lacked respect for them.

'My sister went sort of haywire and my brother went very nasty. If you were in a room with him he would run up to you and punch you, and he would laugh because he thought it was right.'
(CHILD)

● 31% said their children had low self-esteem and 24% thought their children had problems trusting people and forming relationships.

'The kids have been affected by him hitting me all the time… now, if there is a raised voice in the family, my younger daughter shakes, she cries, she runs out of the house . . .I think she has been mentally scarred by it.'
(MOTHER)

'I've always got that picture of my mother in the back of my mind being beaten up, and I think oh, all men are like that, that's going to happen to me.'
(CHILD)

Sources:
[1] Dobash and Dobash, *Violence Against Wives*, Open Books, 1980.
[2] Metropolitan Police service statistics.
[3] Dobash and Dobash, as above.

● The above is a summary of *The Hidden Victims*, a report published by NCH Action for Children. For a copy of the main report, see page 39 for address details.

Children's experiences of living with domestic violence

An extract from *Children's experiences of living with domestic violence*, a collection of papers drawing on practical experience and on research with women and children who have experienced domestic violence

These first-hand accounts from children were gathered by Gina Higgins, a member of the National Child Development Workers Group in Women's Aid Federation England (WAFE). The childworker's strongest impression from doing this work for the book was that it confirmed how, although people often do not talk to children about their experiences and even try to stop them thinking about what they have been through, children benefit enormously from talking to someone they can trust. They often feel caught in the middle between their parents so can find it difficult to talk to either of them. Given the chance to talk to a childworker in a refuge – who is there just for them and who will listen to them and support them – they make tremendous progress and are helped to work on their feelings of anger and sadness.

Thus the work of gathering these accounts actually fed into the work being undertaken with the children and had some positive results, both for them and their mothers.

Boy aged 12, white, ex-resident

When I lived in the refuge I had to share one room with my brother and Mum. It was OK, I didn't mind, you get what you are given. The workers couldn't afford a bigger house. I can't remember much because I was four and a half and now I'm 12 years old.

'I keep in touch with the refuge and sometimes I go when there is a workshop on for us. The best one was about Malcolm X, it was about race awareness. I thought it was interesting and I could write my own thing about him.

'I now live with my Mum and I like it. My Mum has a girlfriend and I like her as well. I like living here. My brother is 16 and lives now with my Dad – I don't mind. I like my school and I have been chosen by my class to be their council representative. I don't see my Dad much; I see him when I want – every two months. My Mum has helped me a lot, she talks to me about racism and sexism and about sexuality and keeping safe.'

Boy aged 14, Asian/Caribbean, ex-resident

'My Dad cut my Mum with a knife; children left and went to Auntie. I was there – I used to hear arguments and shouting about drinking ('Alcoholic!')

'Unhappy I felt – I'd go in my room and play, I was 10 years. Domestic violence is horrible – not worth it, people getting hurt. I never see my Dad – I saw him once one year ago, walking down the street; we just walked on. I don't feel anything for Dad. Relationship better with Mum and me.

'Relationship all right – we fight a bit, me and my brother, and hurt each other. I play a lot with my baby brother. In the refuge I liked the playroom and everything – I felt safe.

'Changed school six times – I got worried: start all over again making friends. School now all right, I know everyone there. I've been there one and a half years, feel better at school – I've friends. Temporary accommodation, we've been accepted for a three bedroom house – feel great! Auntie helped us.

'Watch violent films and start acting them out. It gets out of order: one gets hurt and angry, then we hit each other harder. Family therapy might help us all. We are now going there as a family.'

Boy aged 6,
Asian, resident

'He says he loves my Mum but he lies. He tells Mum to do everything at home. He never gave Mum any money. He hit my Mum, I saw it. I tried to look happy but I wasn't inside. He never played with me – I felt lonely. I feel sad for my Dad, he's an idiot. I do not like my Dad. My Dad hit my sister with a plate and she started bleeding on her head. She was red everywhere.

'I feel happy now, 'cos I'm away from my Dad; he can't find us now because he doesn't know the way.

'I saw my Dad yesterday in a car at my Nan's, shouting 'Us Salaam Alaikum' (a traditional greeting – the equivalent of 'hello'). I was really frightened. I don't feel happy at new school – no friends. We kids make a mess and Mum cleans it up. We're OK now.

'My Dad really wants to kill us and shoot us. He will lock us in a room and we will never get out and have nothing to eat. I must look after my Mum, my Dad is really bad.

'When I am big, I could be Batman and go and kill my Dad and throw him in a dustbin.

'I like the refuge because if children do something wrong you see the workers and then it's all right.

'I am scared when I have to see my Dad sometimes, that he will hurt me and shoot me. He said lots of times he would do that to all of us.'

Boy aged 13,
Asian/Caribbean, ex-resident

'My Dad attacked my Mum with a knife. My Dad cut my Mum's toe. He fell asleep. I was at Auntie's. I saw my Mum and I fainted. He used to hit my brother and me. Felt pretty sad. Domestic violence: I think it's bad that it should happen. Go where they can get help. Dad is abusive, needs mental help. I help Mum so she doesn't get bad memories and my baby brother is OK.

'We arranged to see Dad but he didn't turn up. I felt disappointed.

'It was fun in the refuge. Good for my Mum 'cos other women were in similar situations.

'Relationship is going good, some bad points. I don't listen to her – she gets angry. I try to listen to her

now and help her. We fight a lot and we play too.

'Dad hit my brother a lot and I think my brother takes it out on me 'cos he thought my Dad liked me better. We are in temporary accommodation at the moment. We will be getting a home soon.

'School: I'm doing good, sometimes I don't concentrate. Some friends are a bad influence. Family therapy is helping to stop hitting. I call my brother names so he will hit me. I don't know why I do it. It is abuse as well as my Dad hitting us.'

Girl aged 7,
mixed parentage, ex-resident

'I was really upset sometimes because my Dad; sometimes he hit my Mum and he hit me and my brother, sometimes he could be really nice and we could have lots of fun. It made me feel very unhappy when he hit me, and it hurt. We left and went into a refuge because he was hitting my Mum.

'I'm glad my Mam left and I'm glad I was in the refuge. I have a new life now and new friends

---

'I was scared coming to the refuge at first, but when I met most of the children and played, I was then happy. I liked everything in the refuge. I now live with my Mum and my brother, and my Godmother comes and stays with us sometimes. I feel fine that my Godmother is with us because she is really nice. It's happy in my house now, and Mum and Godmother really understand me most of the time. Me and my brother get on fine; sometimes I can get quite annoyed with him – when we play wrestling he can hurt me, but then he says sorry so that's OK.

'I'm doing very well and I get lots of congratulations for my school work.

'At my Dad's, I wet my knickers by accident and Daddy hit me. I felt scared and unhappy. Sometimes I did not want to see my Dad. I haven't seen my Dad for six weeks now; I feel unhappy because I haven't seen him.

'Sometimes my Dad still threatens my Mum – it makes me feel unhappy. Most of the time they talk about access visits'

'I think no one should do domestic violence ever, even in heaven, because if you go to war you could get hurt or end up dead yourself.'

Girl aged 15,
white, ex-resident

'Me and my Mam and the rest of us left the North and went to live in the refuge. I'm glad my Mam left – it was horrible living at home.

'When we lived in the refuge, I remember the other kids used to take the mick out of my accent. It was OK after, though, because we all had a children's meeting and we were all talking about racism and it came up about languages and accents. I liked the meetings and workshops – all of us learned a lot.

'The room was really small with us all living in it. I was glad when we got our own place. I didn't like travelling to school, though, but I had no choice as I didn't want to leave another school.

'I'm OK about everything now, but my brother had a hard time of it when we moved to our house. He kept bunking off school he said he was being bullied at school. He's OK now, I think!

'I'm glad my Mam left and I'm glad I was in the refuge. I have a new life now and new friends.

'It was wrong for us to live in that situation. I didn't like it when my Mam got hurt and cried. My Dad needs help, like a doctor or someone.

'I am happy now. I have a few problems now, but only little ones. I hope that when I'm older, I won't let a man push me around. My Mam is happy now, and so are we. We never see me Dad now, I like it.'

Children Living with Domestic Violence: Putting Men's Abuse of Women on the Child Care Agenda, edited by Audrey Mullender and Rebecca Morley, Whiting & Birch Ltd, PO Box 872, Forest Hill, London SE23 3HL, £15.95 plus £1.50 p&p.

● The above is an extract from *Childright.*

© *Children's Legal Centre March, 1995*

Violence in the home leaves children in need

Violence in the home causes untold harm to women throughout the country. But what of the harm this violence does to the children? Susan Clark reports

had just been taken away from my Dad. I was frightened that if I told the social worker I was upset about all that had happened to me she would take me away from my Mum. So I kept quiet.'

Social workers are keenly aware of domestic violence. Yet the latest report reveals continuing failure by professionals to grasp the effects the violence has on children.

It Hurts Me Too, published last week by the Women's Aid Federation, Childline and the National Institute for Social Work, demands special training for social workers to raise awareness of the effects, how to recognise them and how to sensitively deal with children's needs. It also calls for better child support.

'They should be classed as children in need under section 17 of the Children Act,' says Thangam Debbonaire, national children's officer of WAFE, and contributor to the report.

Research has shown that domestic violence is the second most common violent crime reported to the police. One in four violent crimes reported is domestic. Yet only 20 per cent of domestic assaults mentioned by women in the 1992 British Crime Survey were said to have been reported to the police. And, according to the Association of London Authorities, one in five murder victims is a woman killed by her current or ex-partner.

Children are often involved. They may witness the incident or overhear it from another room. Worse still they can also be on the receiving end. Of a sample of 130 callers to Childline, collated for the report, 38 per cent said they had been assaulted.

Speaking at a conference on domestic violence and children, organised by NCH Action For Children and NSPCC last week, Liz Kelly of the Child Abuse Unit at the University of North London said

more than half of child protection cases included an element of domestic violence toward the mother.

The report found that short-term effects on children include fear, nervousness, confusion, and longer-term problems such as an inability to make and keep close friends, aggressiveness, lack of concentration, hyperactivity, depression, low self-esteem and eating disorders. Education is also often seriously disrupted.

It Hurts Me Too supports research carried out by NCH Action For Children, published in December last year, when 108 women attending their family centres were interviewed. One in four said their children were aggressive to them, 72 per cent said the children were frightened, 48 per cent that they had become withdrawn and 34 per cent said they wetted the bed.

During the financial year 1993-4, nearly 28,000 children were given shelter in women's refuges in England. But only 75 per cent of the 214 refuges in England have a children's officer.

'There is a danger, because of funding cutbacks by local authorities, of a patchy provision of support for children escaping domestic violence,' said WAFE's Debbonaire. 'The statutory authorities must recognise the need for refuges and children's officers to protect women and their children. They must make funding refuges a priority.'

Jan Pahl, director of research at the NISW, agreed. 'The report underlines the importance of refuges in providing support for women and children and the urgent need for more secure funding for their work.'

© *Community Care*
April, 1995

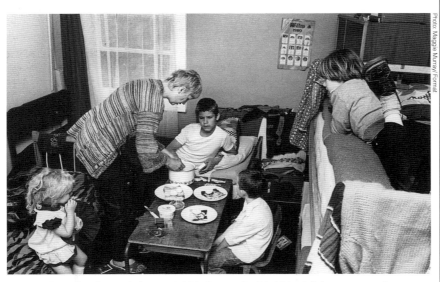

During the financial year 1993-4, nearly 28,000 children were given shelter in women's refuges in England

The problems facing black, Asian and ethnic minority women

Women from Asian, Afro-Caribbean and ethnic minority communities face additional problems when it comes to violent marriages. The cultural tradition of keeping the family together at all costs may well put enormous pressure on you to stick with your husband, whatever his behaviour. In addition, society's institutions may make assumptions about women from ethnic minorities. For instance, Southall Black Sisters, who are based in an area of London with a majority Asian population, say that there is often an assumption that Asian women have 'higher tolerance levels' of domestic violence. They say that Asian women sometimes feel that the police may be unwilling to intervene in domestic disputes within ethnic minority families because they think that the community is 'self-policing'. And not all police stations, GPs' surgeries, hospitals or social services have adequate interpreting facilities for women whose first language is not English. The possibility of facing questions about their immigration status, often deters women from reporting incidents of violence.

Immigration laws mean that you often have to rely on your husband if you want to stay in Britain. The main immigration dilemma for a woman born outside this country is the One Year Rule laid down by the Home Office. It requires you to stay married for at least a year before you are granted 'Given Leave to Stay Indefinitely' status. If your husband is violent, you are faced with an almost impossible choice. If you stay in the marriage, you might put your safety and that of your children at risk. If you leave, your husband can report you are no longer happily married and you could be deported. Back in your country of origin it is possible you will be ostracised by your family and your whole community,

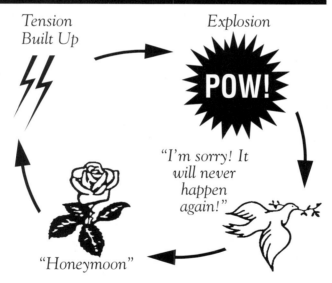

Violence is part of a cycle – it is not a one-off event.

Tension Built Up

Explosion

POW!

"I'm sorry! It will never happen again!"

"Honeymoon"

and may even face violence from them. This is especially so in some cultures, where the concept of family honour will have been violated by the wife leaving her husband.

Without this immigration status, you can't claim Social Security. You won't be entitled to claim Housing Benefit (which refuges rely on to keep going), although you should still be accepted into a women's refuge. Other minority communities have their own cultural expectations. For instance, women in the Jewish community face the problem of having to keep up the myth that there is never any friction in Jewish families. This has meant an enormous reluctance by women to report violence to the police. In Orthodox families the great emphasis on having lots of children means a woman is more financially dependent on her husband, and less likely to leave while her children are growing up.

Case history

Surinder is 32 and has three daughters:

'I came over from India for an arranged marriage in 1981. I loved my husband a lot and after two years I gave birth to a daughter. That was when the beatings started. Then I had another child – again a girl. There is enormous pressure to have a boy. In Asian families girls are nothing. I had to cope with his family taunting me and calling me 'useless' because I hadn't given him a son. In between all this I had to work in the family shop from 9am to 11pm as well as raising two children and cooking for his family. Back home I had a degree but no one wanted to know about that here. The third baby was born in 1988 – again a girl. For the first six months of her life my husband never even came near her. My life seemed so pointless that I tried to kill myself twice; I was so worn down by his verbal abuse and beating. Soon after my husband took us all to India on the pretext of a four-week holiday.

He went off one day and left us there – no passports, no papers, nothing. He said he'd kill me if I returned to England. Then he went back. We were stranded for two years and only came home because my brother paid for the tickets. When I got back my husband filed for divorce because he wanted a son. I never wanted to associate my name with a divorce because, in my culture, it brings you and your family huge shame. You are treated with contempt; the thinking is that when a marriage fails it's always the woman's fault. Yet it was my husband who was the violent and unfaithful one. We divorced in 1992, and now he's re-married and has a son. I have nothing – no family, no support, and no money. He took my parents' dowry money when we married, plus all my jewellery. I'm trying to get it back, but I don't have much hope.'

Case history:

Ibilola, a 33 year-old Nigerian mother of two, came to Britain to marry a man she'd met back in Nigeria. Within a year the marriage had broken down: 'He gave me cigarette burns, he beat me and destroyed all mine and the children's clothes. When I called the police and they came round, the first thing they wanted to know was whether I was legally allowed to stay in the UK. That was more important to them than how badly injured I was. Eventually I left, but then I went back for the children's sake and because I wanted to try again. But after two years I was back in the refuge. My husband told me he had the law on his side because he is British and he could do anything to me. I'm from a small village and it didn't occur to me to question what he was saying.'

When her husband went to the Home Office, Ibilola was threatened with deportation. Now her status is verified and she is allowed to stay.

See page 39 for information on refuges and advice for black, Asian and ethnic minority women.

The above is an extract from *'When Home is Where the Hurt is'* produced by the BBC Radio Two Social Action Team.

© BBC Radio Two

Key principles

From Refuge

Assaulting a woman in the home is a criminal offence, equal to, if not worse than, assault on the street.

No man has the right to inflict injury on a woman for any reason or at any time.

Men who batter their wives or partners are responsible for their own behaviour; violence is not their only choice in reacting to domestic problems.

Assaulted women are not responsible for the violence. They do not derive any pleasure from being physically hurt or threatened. Battering is a social crime which cuts across all classes, religions and ethnic groups.

The roots of domestic assault lie in social conditioning. It is society's responsibility to provide women with protection from abuse and to insist that the appropriate laws are enforced to prevent violence and not to condone it.

Women have been conditioned from birth to consider themselves subservient to, and dependent on, the will of a man.

Being a victim of emotional and/or physical abuse is not a reflection on a battered woman's character or her worth as a human being. A battered woman must be supported by helping her to regain confidence and self-esteem so that she can explore her options and take her own decisions.

At Refuge, we can give her confidence to start new lives for herself and her children to become her own person.

Training of professionals helps to expel the myths of domestic violence, expose assault as unacceptable behaviour and ensure that a woman is not being denied her human rights.

What we as Agencies have to do is to fight the ignorance that shrouds the subject of domestic violence in myth and stereotype.

Raising public awareness, together with an integrated approach in working with the police, health workers and other social agencies, is essential to effective progress.

'Police officers are reminded …where there is evidence that a non-arrestable offence as been committed, an arrest may be necessary "to protect a child or other vulnerable person".' Metropolitan Police Force Order, June 1987

© Refuge

Why I had to find Beth and Mandy guilty

By Phil Redmond

Brookside's best-kept secret has provoked a national outcry as Mandy and Beth Jordache were found guilty of murdering Mandy's abusive husband Trevor. Immediately after the verdict was transmitted on Tuesday, viewers, lobby groups and the media began calling Channel 4 and ourselves at Mersey TV to protest that the verdict was 'wrong'.

We made particular efforts to maximise the impact of this storyline because of the importance of the issues. Working to the theory that the best way to keep a secret is to tell so many secrets no one knows which is the truth, we shot two different versions of the verdict – and seven weeks following it. The resulting uproar – including a demonstration outside our offices yesterday by the local Campaign Against Domestic Violence – is no surprise to me. Brookside has a history of radicalism and innovation. What has been remarkable has been the way the fictional story has become entwined with the perceived shortcomings of Britain's legal system.

The two principal points of the storyline were to highlight the difficult legal position in which women like Mandy Jordache find themselves, and the fact that the British legal system is not based on the fantasies of Hollywood.

It would have been extremely easy to claim dramatic licence and, after a few courtroom histrionics, provide the fairy-tale ending. Indeed, the day before transmission we faced great pressure to respond to many pleas for a 'not guilty' verdict. Yet after months of research involving charities and women's groups, different legal counsel, and finally a High Court judge, the most realistic and probable verdict was that as transmitted. In the eyes of the law, as it currently stands, the characters are guilty and the judge has no discretion. The mandatory sentence for murder is life.

The point of this verdict was to continue the debate on the very important issues of the definition of 'provocation', diminished responsibility and the degree of murder itself. Is it right that a man can kill after years of nagging by a wife and be sentenced to manslaughter – whereas a woman who waits a mere 60 seconds after another beating is judged to have acted with premeditation?

These, of course, are not issues that a television fiction can resolve. What we can do through television drama is create a climate, however fleeting, that pushes the issue to the forefront of public consciousness and therefore hopefully provides a more sympathetic climate for campaigners.

To do this we had to show the judicial process as accurately as we could. This even extended to different lighting techniques to add a stark reality to the courtroom. Judging by the calls, faxes, letters and media exposure received, it would appear that we have at least achieved the aim of highlighting the issue.

The verdict of guilty was both legally credible and probable. It also allows us to continue to support the debate about domestic violence for a good many months to come. But Brookside is, after all, a piece of fiction. The aim of the programme is to entertain – and initial overnight figures suggest Tuesday's episode achieved the programme's highest share of audience in its 12-year history. This popular support for a drama which is tackling one of the most disturbing and intractable of social problems also tells us something about the millions of viewers who tuned in to watch and were moved by the verdict.

Ever since Dickens sealed the fate of Little Nell, serialised fiction has demonstrated a remarkable capacity to reach out to enormous audiences. Brookside – in its own way – demonstrated on Tuesday the cumulative power of a story told serially – in this case over a period of two years.

Other dramas will draw bigger audiences. But the advantage of Brookside is that it can single-mindedly focus on an issue which enters into a national debate. In the case of the Jordache trial, it seems to have reinvigorated a debate about an important subject. Yet, there is something disturbing about the capacity of a television story to provoke a debate which seems entirely to have passed by politicians and other pundits who remain so Westminster-focused that they often appear no longer to notice the really big questions facing people on a daily basis.

Behind that indifference may also be an ignorance of the legal system and the sense of injustice many women are forced to suffer. Domestic violence, the way the legal system is obliged to treat such cases, and the wider issues of availability of resources such as a national helpline for victims and safe houses and other forms of support, ought to be at the forefront of any government's policy-making agenda.

Perhaps one reason why our guilty verdict touched so many raw nerves was because in confronting the apparently 'real' fate of Mandy Jordache, many people watching will have realised they too are guilty – not of murder, but of indifference to the fate of women like Mandy. Let us hope that many of these issues can be addressed in the not too distant future.

© *The Guardian*
May, 1995

Battered men come out of the closet

Domestic violence is not confined to men against women; men abuse men too. Nick Kirby reports

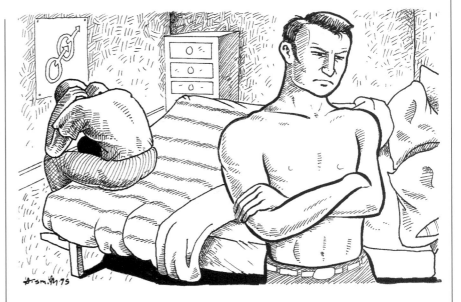

While the subject of battered women is depressingly familiar, we rarely hear of battered men. It is not just that men are supposed to be strong: gay domestic violence is a taboo subject. Victims feel, with some justification, that they will be the subject of disbelief and ridicule by the police, the legal system and society at large.

There is also denial within the gay community itself – beleaguered groups are often unwilling to wash their dirty linen in public. Yet American studies suggest that violence within same-sex relationships is in proportion to heterosexual relationships (though precise figures are impossible to obtain).

Understanding the causes of gay men's domestic violence is tricky, simply because of a lack of research in this country.

However, in their book *Men Who Beat the Men Who Love Them* (Haworth), David Island and Patrick Letellier stress that there is a distinct pattern of violence, based on a warped assertion of power, common both to same-sex and to heterosexual domestic violence.

At the start of the relationship, everything appears perfect; then, gradually, the batterer will start to show violent behaviour, which tends to increase in severity. The trigger may be alcohol- or drug-related or it may be nothing more than a bad day at the office.

Violent incidents almost always occur suddenly, and without prelude. This usually puts the victim on a knife-edge, not knowing when violence will break out. And it is rare for violence to take place in public; to most observers, the relationship may seem quite normal. It is rare for the batterer to be violent with people outside the relationship: he sticks to an established territory, where he has built up control over a considerable period.

Physical violence is only one aspect of the abuse that may take place. Island and Letellier define gay men's domestic violence as 'any unwanted physical force, psychological abuse, material or property destruction, inflicted on one man by another'.

Still, in all battering relationships, a time will come when the victim finds he has to escape from his assailant. In some cases, it may be a matter of life or death. But how does he do this? In very few cases of gay men's domestic violence will it be possible for the victim simply to walk away from the batterer and never see him again.

Unfortunately, there are no organisations or helplines that deal specifically with this phenomenon, as they do for battered heterosexuals and battered lesbians. There are, however, organisations that can and do advise gay men on domestic violence, such as the London Lesbian and Gay switchboard and Survivors (an organisation originally set up to help victims of male rape).

The advice that these helplines give may be extremely valuable, but sometimes the only recourse is to take legal action. Unfortunately, this is hard for the victim. As solicitor Simon Woods points out: 'There is no legislation in place to protect same-sex couples from domestic violence. The only remedy a victim has is to take action for assault, battery, trespass or nuisance in County Court, during the course of which injunctions can be obtained to restrain the other party from further acts of assault.'

And, indicative of the difficulties facing victims, Mr Woods continues: 'We do receive inquiries. But they usually don't get very far because people often change their minds.'

A County Court injunction can cost anything up to £800 and may be enforceable for only three months. Hardly surprising, then, that Mr Woods reports: 'For the most part, this kind of litigation is very rare. People are worried about going to the police because they don't think they will be taken seriously.'

The situation is beginning to change. Last year, London's Hammersmith and Shepherd's Bush police divisions targeted same-sex domestic violence and included it in the newly formed Domestic Violence and Community Support Units (DVCSUs) – confidential, plain-clothed specialist support teams.

However, these units are still in their infancy. Stephanie Knight, of the Hammersmith DVCSU, says: 'There has not been a great response so far, and the vast majority of incidents go unreported.' She also feels that there is a 'real lack of training to deal with the different dynamics within same-sex relationships'.

There is a long way to go in bringing gay men's domestic violence out of the closet. The gay community must overcome its denial, and the rest of society has to confront its prejudices and stereotypes.

There is a domestic violence Bill due to be put before the Commons later this year, which includes an extended category covering 'associated household members'. The Law Commission has indicated that this may cover same-sex relationships. The lesbian and gay lobbying organisation Stonewall is pressing hard for clarification and will table amendments should same-sex relationships not be included in it. Without a doubt, this recognition will be an important step forward in dealing with this frightening issue.

© *The Independent*
April, 1995

Battered husbands afraid to seek help

By Victoria Macdonald

Researchers have uncovered horrific tales of violence by women against men during a study into the 'hidden' problem of battered husbands.

The study by John Moores University in Liverpool 'surprised and horrified' the researchers, who had set out believing there would be only a small number of cases.

Instead, they have been inundated with calls from husbands wanting to tell their stories. Even though the seven-month study has now finished, they are still being contacted.

Sean Stitt and Audrey Macklin, of the university's Centre for Consumer Education and Research, spoke only to men from Merseyside but now want to conduct a nationwide study to encourage the police and social workers to take the problem seriously.

The 20 men finally chosen for the research revealed an appalling catalogue of violence. One man had his hand pinned to a kitchen table with a knife, another had scalding water poured over his face, while a number of others were hit with a variety of implements, including the proverbial rolling pin.

Yet when Dr Stitt and Miss Macklin approached social workers to discuss the way the violence against males was dealt with, they came across what they could only describe as 'anti-male sexism'.

'They adopted an ultra-loony feminist argument of men getting a taste of their own medicine,' Dr Stitt said, 'They had a totally sniggering attitude towards our research.'

Dr Stitt now believes the numbers are higher than previously suspected but the stigma of being a battered man was preventing males from seeking help. When they did, there was little advice or support for them.

'Male victims take steps to cover evidence of their abuse and violence by completely isolating themselves,' he said.

Looking at why the women attacked their male partners, the researchers found a mixture of factors, including alcohol abuse and pre-menstrual tension. But in the vast majority of cases there was either no identifiable cause or there had been a change in the relationship, such as the man losing his job.

The common feature was the woman accusing her husband of 'not being a real man' or being a 'wimp'.

'They become socialised into believing they are not real men and that they should not respond by seeking help,' Dr Stitt said. 'In many cases, they stay in the marriage because they are afraid for their children'.

Roger Williams, of the pressure group 'Families Need Fathers', attempted to set up a refuge for husbands and their children but was forced to shelve the idea 'because of the judiciary'.

'Men were being told to stay away from us because it would affect their cases,' he said.

'This is not a battered wives versus battered husbands debate. This is about recognising that it is not only women who are suffering from this form of abuse.'

© *The Sunday Telegraph*
January, 1995

The battered male?

By Victoria Freedman

Are men greater victims of violence in the home than women? Has a 'domestic violence industry' grown up which has grossly exaggerated the extent to which women are beaten by their male partners?

Such was the thrust of a recent polemic in the British media, co-authored by Neil Lyndon, writer, social commentator and critic of aspects of feminism. His argument hinged on a recent Mori survey, commissioned and published by the BBC programme 'Here and Now', which showed that, while 5 per cent of women living with men had experienced an incident of violence from those same men, 11 per cent of men living with women said they too had experienced violence from the women they lived with.

This was coupled with a report published in the *Los Angeles Times* to the effect that American men were nine times less likely than women to seek the protection of the police against a violent partner in their own home. While these assertions fly in the face of 20 years of worldwide feminist, academic and government research, and while refuges here and in Britain are bulging at the seams with women fleeing violent partners, Lyndon's controversial piece, written with Paul Ashton, still throws up a question worth looking at. Could the battered man, battered physically – or mentally – be a hidden phenomenon in a world which even today still predominantly expects the male of the species to be macho?

For Les Davidson, who last year set up a helpline in Britain for male victims, the answer to that question is very much 'Yes'.

'It's happening right across the board, from builders to doctors. Such things as pre-menstrual syndrome and post-natal depression have been identified as possibly making women aggressive. Or, in the same way that men are aggressive, it could be as a result of family life, role models, the concealment of abuse or stress at work.'

Davidson began to work in the area of domestic violence in the 1970s when refuges were first set up in Britain.

'I was, and still am, absolutely appalled by what men do to women. But a few years ago I began to get calls from men too. I know it's hard to believe.

I now see domestic violence as a social issue, not a gender issue

Society has given men a role in which they are not acknowledged as victims. If a woman slaps a man, society gives her an excuse for her actions. But should a man slap a woman, he's a batterer.'

Instead of using physical strength, as men do, he says women use weapons but with the same systematic violence which ensures unseen injuries.

'Most injuries to men are to the back of the shoulder, with women using mainly kitchen equipment like knives and scissors. Hot liquid is poured on to the lap. There are a lot of attacks to the genital area.'

He also hears of the accompanying mental cruelty which has been identified as a major part of domestic violence.

'The pattern of abuse involves control and removing your partner's self-esteem. Everybody has the ability to do that, men and women. I now see domestic violence as a social issue, not a gender issue.'

With regard to the Mori survey, another piece of research in the US with similar findings was, however, later totally, refuted by leading British experts Russell and Rebecca Dobash.

Dr Harry Ferguson, from the Department of Social Studies at Trinity College, Dublin, who has worked in the area of violence within the family for the past 17 years – in research, teaching and on a practical level – regards claims that women do not suffer extensive abuse in the home as part of a male backlash.

He was horrified by the Lyndon/Ashton standpoint, which suggested, among other things, that some feminists, the police and workers in women's refuges were set to gain from the amplification of the battered woman issue as the more the public and politicians heard about it, the more money would be poured into tackling the problem.

Harry Ferguson is not prepared to accept that money is being pumped into what Lyndon termed a domestic violence industry and adds: 'The level of services in this country is pathetic.'

There are no official statistics about domestic violence in Ireland, but in the Dublin area alone last year there were 5,000 calls to the Garda unit which was set up in 1993 to deal with women and child abuse. There were also 6,000 calls to the Women's Aid helpline. In 1993, 119 women treated in the casualty unit of St James's Hospital in Dublin admitted they had been victims of domestic violence, suffering from injuries that ranged from multiple bruising to lacerations and fractures. Only one man complained he was a victim of his partner's violence – although she had been previously treated three times.

From these figures, and reports from refuges that they constantly have to send women away due to lack of space, the level of abuse against women in Ireland is horrifying.

However, if there are men here who are victims, Les Davidson would like to hear from them.

Running from pain

Many women leave home to escape violence. Where they can go, and the help they can expect, differs according to their local authority, as Lucie Carrington discovers

Up to 45,000 women a year flee to the safety of a refuge in a bid to escape violence at home. A further 100,000 seek the outreach advice and counselling services many refuges provide. These findings from research carried out for the Women's Aid Federation show the urgent need for refuge services for women and their children. But the same research suggests that few local authorities are prepared to finance these services, or even have a policy for dealing with domestic violence. On average 37 per cent of refuge income comes from local authorities.

Mog Ball, author of the research, says authorities fail to give priority to refuges because they believe users of the services are from outside the area. This highlights a pressing need for a national network of refuge services with perhaps a single agency which brings together and administers all statutory resources.

Local authorities which fund refuges tend to split their support between housing and social services. Housing departments contribute 26 per cent and social services 15 per cent. Other departments may contribute as well. This often results in confusion, leaving departments sympathetic but 'hamstrung by the lack of clear statutory responsibility'. Above all, an effective response to domestic violence requires inter-agency co-ordination at senior policy level.

In Northamptonshire, the chief executive, director of social services, director of education and the local chief constable have set up a high level 'interdependency group', aimed at tackling the problems caused by domestic violence. 'A year ago they concluded domestic violence was extremely expensive to the system. Since then they have done a lot to get people together,' Ball said.

The London Borough of Islington is also taking domestic violence seriously. Davina James-Hanman is the borough's domestic violence co-ordinator. Not attached to housing or social services, she works as part of the women's equality unit which is part of the chief executive's office. 'This allows me to work with every department in the council and talk to all levels and grades. It also gives me and domestic violence a high political profile,' James-Hanman said.

She has been in post for two-and-a-half years. The job was originally funded by a Home Office safer cities project but once that money ran out the council took over the funding. James Hanman knows of only one other similar local authority co-ordinator's position in Greenwich which was set up a few months ago.

Her job is a mixture of policy development, research, education and training and information-giving. She has drawn up guidelines for women who find themselves in violent relationships, which front-line workers give to clients they know are coping with violence. She also provides training for people working with clients who have been subject to violence at home, and now runs a training for trainers course.

Islington accepts women with children fleeing domestic violence as a priority need, and accepts single women escaping violence in the home.

It provides temporary accommodation through two refuges, one of which is solely for Latin American women. It also provides an emergency refuge for single women and longer-term homes for women who are able to leave the support and company of the refuge. The council has devoted 20 homes specifically for rehousing victims of domestic violence.

As well as providing accommodation, which includes for disabled women, the refuge services, in line with others, provide counselling and support to help women deal with their financial and emotional needs. And it employs a child care worker to work on a one-to-one basis with abused children.

Money for the refuges comes directly from the social services budget. Residents' housing benefit, as in other refuges, also contributes funds. But the council does not run the homes – that is done through voluntary management committees.

Hereford & Worcester County Council is not as advanced as Islington but takes domestic violence seriously enough to provide core funding for its purpose-built refuge services, and employs a liaison officer, Lyn Hazel.

Hazel oversees training in domestic violence – often this means experienced workers in the refuges help train other agencies. But the children's workers are expected to come to training sessions on child protection and this is included in service agreement.

In some authorities, liaison may mean a policing role, but Hazel said relations between the refuge and the local authority are good enough for her not to worry whether they are fulfilling their contract. This is partly because Hazel is a volunteer at the refuge committed to its success and independence.

This is a theme the Women's Aid Federation likes to hammer home. It is vital refuges remain independent from the social services and housing departments, even if that is where they get most of their funding. Women using them must feel they are in a safe environment. The way round this is for refuges to ensure they do not get all their money from the local authority. But Hazel is aware that core funding has to come from the council.

This is the biggest question mark hanging over refuges, even in authorities such as Hereford & Worcester which have a positive approach to domestic violence. The axe hanging over so many jobs and services is hanging over them too, making the Women's Aid Federation's call for a £50 million investment in services increasingly unlikely.

Some of the myths of woman abuse

Woman abuse only affects certain social groups.
Wrong. Titles and university degrees do not eliminate family violence. A grim proportion of families hiding this secret are among the professions.

Every family has a row once in a while.
Women and children arrive at Refuge with fractured skulls, knife wounds and burns as well as bruises. A man does not have the right to cause bodily harm to a person because he is in a bad temper. Often there is no argument, just assault.

It's the woman's fault.
Untrue. Violence is a crime. She is the victim, not the criminal. When woman assault becomes publicly known (perhaps because the woman has been killed by it) the batterer will usually claim that he has been provoked. But no provocation justifies using physical abuse to intimidate partners. A man may earn the privilege of sharing a woman's life but he can never be entitled to own, control or punish her.

Woman assault is a private matter we shouldn't interfere with.
Wrong. Violence is a crime. After being bullied, a woman is in no state to fight for her rights as a human being. She needs our help. Too many women are being prevented by violence from playing their part in the world. The effects on the children are miserable and can be disastrous. There can be no doubt that when we reduce woman abuse we will reduce child abuse.

There are surely not that many cases of domestic violence?
There are. Woman battering occurs throughout our society, probably in one in ten relationships, even though they may appear normal. 25 per cent of all reported violent crime is woman assault (Women's Aid statistic). It is so widespread that the only answer must be in educating all of us. The lesson is that no man has the right to keep his wife/partner in line.

It's the drink that does it.
This is a popular myth. Assaults are also committed by sober men Alcohol can aggravate the problem but it does not cause it.

What about the battered men then?
Male abuse can exist (we have known one case), but it is very, very rare. Men are usually physically stronger and more ready to use force.

The women must be masochists or they would not stay so long.
Manifestly untrue. When a bullying man brainwashes his partner into feeling that she is worthless without him, too much of our world stands behind him. Many women feel they are solely responsible for the happiness of the home and leaving is an admission of failure. They have nowhere to go. Housing and social security officers can play 'Catch 22' about helping. Police do not have time or understanding enough to protect them. Leaving may mean abandoning all her possessions and her entire way of life. If it wasn't for organisations like Refuge, they would have nowhere to go.

What can a woman expect from Women's Aid?

If you are putting a woman in touch with Women's Aid you will want to give her as clear a picture as possible of our organisation and what will happen to her when she approaches us.

Firstly, it should be made clear to her that any approach she makes to us will be totally confidential, and at least initially she can remain anonymous if she so wishes. It should be emphasised that she need not be seeking actual refuge accommodation in order to make use of our organisation. A large part of our work involves giving information to abused women about their legal position, about social security, housing, etc. We realise how difficult it is for a woman to decide what is the best solution for herself and her children, and we simply try to provide her with the information she needs in order to come to a decision. It should also be emphasised that she will not be rushed into making a decision. However, if she decides that she does want refuge accommodation, she would have less time to deliberate as there are always many women in need of refuge accommodation. A space can only be kept open for a particular woman for a limited period of time. Having said that, a woman who decides not to make use of a refuge space on one occasion should feel no hesitation about contacting Women's Aid in the future. Some women may want to have the man excluded under the Matrimonial Homes Act, and Women's Aid could support them in this.

What is refuge life like?

Refuges vary in terms of type and size of building. Some are ordinary three-bedroomed council houses in a housing scheme, some are in tenements within a city, and some are six-bedroomed detached houses. They are not hostels and every effort is made to make them as much like a home as possible. Kitchen, toilet and living-room facilities are shared and usually a woman would be given a bedroom for herself and her children, although in an emergency a woman might be asked to share with someone else. There are no wardens in the refuges and the women make their own decisions about how they want to organise cooking arrangements, keeping the refuge clean, etc. Regular contact is maintained between the Women's Aid group and the refuge by fairly frequent visits by paid and/ or unpaid workers.

What will the other women be like?

The women who come to our refuges come from a cross-section of society. Many of them have had doubts before coming to the refuge about the 'kind of woman' they will be sharing with, or the difficulties which they feel there might be in sharing with other people. What we usually find is that, because the women have been through a similar experience, they give each other tremendous support in practical and emotional terms. Obviously, difficulties can arise, or there can be personality clashes or tensions arising from people living together in a difficult situation, and women are encouraged to speak about their difficulties openly and to try to resolve the situation among themselves. Many women have made lasting friendships with others they have met in the refuges.

How safe are the refuges?

Every effort is made to keep the location of refuges secret as we are well aware of the fear that women

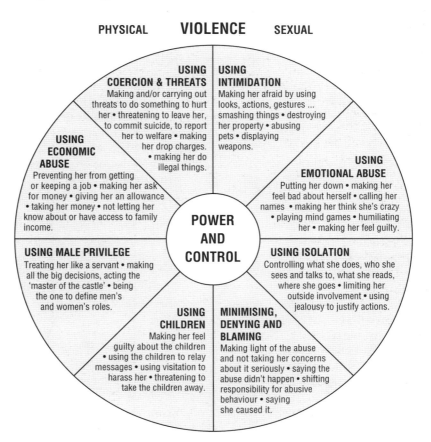

have that the men will find out where they are. It is impressed upon children how important it is that they should tell no-one the address of the refuge. If a man contacted Women's Aid asking for information about a woman or saying that he wanted to see her, we would always consult the woman before even acknowledging that she was in touch with us, and she would then make her own decision about contacting him.

The local police station is always notified as to the whereabouts of the refuge, and the police are usually very helpful if there are any difficulties with regard to men at the refuge. Each refuge has a telephone with which they can contact either the police or Women's Aid workers. Although there have been instances of men finding out the address of a refuge, a very small proportion of men ever actually turn up there. There is also the added security in a refuge of a woman knowing that she is not alone – there are other sympathetic people around to help.

If a woman is too afraid to go to a refuge in her own town, then Women's Aid can arrange for her to move outside her local area altogether, so that she can feel safe.

What about the children?

If a woman decides that she does want to leave with her children, she is encouraged to bring them with her to the refuge, as opposed to waiting till a later date for them to join her. Schools in the locality of the refuge are generally most helpful, and will take children from the refuges at very short notice. Many of the refuges have playrooms and children's workers, and we encourage unpaid workers with a particular interest in young people to spend time with the children; although each woman has responsibility for her own child/ children.

Women often express fears about how the upheaval of leaving home will affect the children, but in fact most of the children have already suffered at home because of the atmosphere (even if they have not actually witnessed violence), and only start to readjust when the stress they have been under at home is removed.

Scottish Women's Aid is there to help groups respond adequately to the needs of children whose mothers come to Women's Aid for help.

© Scottish Women's Aid
March, 1995

Domestic violence and medical services

From Northern Ireland Women's Aid Federation

It appears, however, that having sufficiently overcome feelings of shame and fears of reprisal by their spouses to visit their GPs, women, once there, find it difficult to approach the subject of domestic violence directly. Again feelings of shame seemed to prevent them making direct admissions of the causes of their injuries.*

General practitioners have the first and a 24-hour responsibility for their patient's health care – women who are subject to domestic violence also go to hospitals for treatment, both as in patients and as out patients. Many more fail to seek medical help, usually because they are too ashamed or are intimidated by a partner who will not allow them to involve outside help.

Who can help?

General Medical Practitioners
Women who are victims of domestic violence are more likely to visit their GP than any other helping profession although they do not always state the reason for the visit. Some women may feel that a kind of 'stigma' is attached to a visit to any other agency, such as the police or social services, and that a visit to the doctor is almost sure to be confidential. Many women turn to their GP with an associated problem; therefore the GP is in a prime position to identify the domestic violence problem and many women report that they have had great help and support from their GP. There are, however, some difficulties.

Problem areas in treating domestic violence

Women often minimise, deny or attempt to hide the abuse and its results, and quite often will present with a variety of symptoms: depression, headaches, backache, or sleeping difficulties, or they may present with a child who wets the bed or has other emotional problems.

The motivation for covering up ranges from embarrassment, to fear that their partner (who may also be a patient) could discover their 'disloyalty' in revealing the truth to somebody else. An expectation that the doctor does not want to hear about their relationship problem may prevent a woman from asking for help.

Many GPs do not consider it their role to be that of a 'marriage guidance counsellor' and prefer to restrict themselves to 'real medical issues'.

The average appointment lasts between six and ten minutes, not normally long enough for a sensitive and thorough counselling session. Such 'doctor-centred' consultations may serve to discourage women from disclosing their abuse. The 'by the way' comment is common, whereby the patient mentions or hints at the true reason, and usually towards the end of the appointment. Doctors may not welcome these confessions. Discovery of deeper problems may take up too much time. Many GPs feel the solutions lie outside their field. They may not know how to deal with this problem.

It is widely accepted that GPs in the past provided tranquillisers, as a quick solution to a patient's problems, instead of getting to the root of the anxiety. A busy doctor, lacking time and training for counselling, may fall easily into the trap of prescribing inappropriately.

Health visitors

Health visitors are nurses who are especially trained for work in the community. Their main aim is to promote good health and to offer advice and support. They also liaise between their clients and other services. The bulk of their responsibility is for children under five.

The health visitor plays a crucial role in that she can make regular visits to all families. Because health visitors attend the 'general' population, their calls do not carry any stigma and are open ended. Many women do confide in a health visitor during routine visits. Unlike a GP who is consulted only when a woman chooses to go to the surgery, health visitors are in a perfect position to follow up any concerns regarding domestic violence.

How health visitors can help

Women who have left home because of violence worry that they will be blamed for uprooting the family, and that they will be blamed for the violence.

The worries may focus on fears that Social Services will be given information and that the children could be taken into care if she is failing to cope. Health visitors are in a good position to allay such fears, and they should be aware that women in crisis often do not cope as well as usual and provide additional support necessary to see the mother through the crisis.

Hospitals

Women visit the accident and emergency departments in hospitals either by choice or in order that their own GP will not know – or out of necessity in a medical emergency, including suicide attempts.

Casualty departments are usually crowded with long queues. Staff there are usually stretched, and many would – until recently – have little specialised training. There have been some changes regarding this with nursing staff.

Normally, only the immediate injury is treated. Details of the injury and the alleged reason for the injury will be noted. This information may prove useful in future court cases.

Women who are admitted into hospital overnight are more likely to receive extra attention. This usually takes the form of a referral to the hospital's Social Services department, and whether she is followed up or not will depend on the woman's response. Since casualty may be the first and only request for help, the response for victims of domestic violence is critical. The nursing and medical staff can help by being aware of the problem, and making themselves familiar with the different agencies that can offer the support and advice the women need. They can also check if it is safe for the woman to return home.

Casualty departments normally display posters and telephone numbers of helping agencies. Many referrals come to Women's Aid from this source.

* Home Office Research Study: 107

© Northern Ireland Women's Aid Federation, June 1995

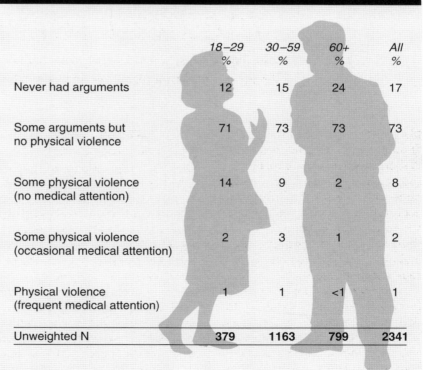

Women's lifetime experience of domestic violence
(during past and present relationships)

	18–29 %	30–59 %	60+ %	All %
Never had arguments	12	15	24	17
Some arguments but no physical violence	71	73	73	73
Some physical violence (no medical attention)	14	9	2	8
Some physical violence (occasional medical attention)	2	3	1	2
Physical violence (frequent medical attention)	1	1	<1	1
Unweighted N	379	1163	799	2341

Notes:

1 Source: 1992 BCS Follow-up A core sample: } don't knows' (n = 12) and 'refusals' (n = 11 on marital status and n = 9 on violence question) excluded.

2 Includes only women aged 18 or over who have been married or lived with a partner.

© Home Office Research and Statistics Department

Do you need legal protection against violence?

From Welsh Women's Aid

This article tells you about ways to use the law to protect you against violence in your own home. While covering the main points, it is not a substitute for a solicitor's advice, which we recommend you seek. Please also read our leaflet *'What Can I Expect From the Police'* which explains about pressing criminal charges.

Where do I start?

Taking any legal action can be complicated. You'll need help and support.

The first step is to contact your local Women's Aid group. They may suggest an experienced solicitor and offer you other information and practical support you may need. Using the law is usually only one aspect of protecting yourself.

I don't want to prosecute, just to feel safe. What can I do?

You can ask a court for an order to protect you under the civil law. There are various different orders which are available to married and unmarried women.

Don't be discouraged by all the different names of the orders, or the different laws that you can use. It's your solicitor's job to understand all that.

An order is a legal instruction given by a judge or magistrates telling your partner not to hit you, molest you or threaten you or your children with physical, mental or sexual abuse.

The court can also order a violent partner to leave the house or the surrounding area. It can also order that you be allowed back into your home and/or to remain there. You don't have to be the owner or tenant.

If you are being abused by someone else e.g. your son or father-in-law a solicitor can advise you of available legal remedies.

What about my children?

If necessary, an order may be made which covers your children. You need to discuss this with your solicitor and Women's Aid group.

If you are afraid that your children may be harmed or snatched, there are legal steps you can take to protect them. Other adults who have been important to the children may also do this.

If you have to leave home without your children, it is absolutely essential to seek legal advice immediately.

Will I have to pay to go to court?

The Legal Aid scheme can help you to pay, either for a solicitor's advice only (which is called Green Form advice), or for legal proceedings.

If you are on Income Support, you will not have to pay at all in the first instance – but make sure that you understand the circumstances in which the Legal Aid Board can expect to be repaid (Women's Aid can help you with this).

Legal Aid can be granted very quickly – this is called Emergency Legal Aid. Your solicitor will have to work hard to convince the Legal Aid Board that Emergency Legal Aid is necessary, so it is very important that you have a solicitor who is experienced in, and committed to, this type of action.

How soon will I go to court?

In an emergency case, you could go to court the same day or very shortly afterwards without your partner being there. An order may then be made which lasts for a short period and you would need to return to court when it expired.

At an emergency hearing the court are unlikely to make an order telling someone to leave the house without hearing their side of the story.

Otherwise, you will probably have to wait days or weeks, and your partner will be summoned to attend court. If he does not turn up, the court will proceed without him as long as he has received a copy of the court papers.

What is it like in court?

It you are worried about it, talk about the day with Women's Aid before you go. It can be an ordeal, so ask a friend or Women's Aid worker to come with you to support you. This might be the first time that you have had to face your violent partner again.

Talk to your solicitor to find out what to expect and what the court is like. Many courts have very inadequate waiting facilities. You may need to take a flask and sandwiches and be prepared for a long wait.

Will I have to tell the court everything?

The courts usually hear these cases in private. You will need to prepare a written statement (called an affidavit) describing past assaults or threats made to you/your children by your partner and when and where they took place.

In court you may be asked to say that the content of the affidavit is true and provide any clarification or updating that is necessary. Your solicitor will tell you this beforehand.

Evidence from your doctor, hospital, the police, witnesses and photographs of your injuries can all help your case.

It can be a very painful exercise to describe your experiences in such detail, but a good affidavit is very important to your case. Before working on the final version with your solicitor, your local Women's Aid group may help you to prepare this written evidence in a supportive atmosphere. Many of us have had similar experiences.

Is an order effective as soon as the court makes it?

No. An order has to be served on the person to whom it applies. If the court case is taken in an emergency or if you expect that your partner might not turn up, you may need to supply the court with some information that will help to find him.

Therefore, go prepared with his photograph, likely addresses, details of his job or where and when he signs on and any other regular activities.

What must I do next?

Ensure that you have a copy of the order and keep it with you at all times. A copy of the order should be available to your local police. This is not your responsibility, but it's worth asking your solicitor to check that your local police station is aware of the order.

If the order affects your children, inform the head teacher and their class teacher.

If you don't understand the order, ask your solicitor to explain it to you. If there is a 'power of arrest' attached, does it cover all the conditions of the order or just some?

Does the order prohibit all the actions of your partner that would make you afraid?

Your partner may bring gifts and try to move back in, talk to you or approach you outside the children's school, but if you allow him to come into the house, or talk to him, you may be breaching the order yourself. This will make it very difficult to get a subsequent breach of the order taken seriously.

How long will the order last?

Most orders are for three months, but this varies. They are designed as short-term solutions to a crisis situation which you can use as a 'breathing space' to consider your options for the future. You will probably need the support of Woman's Aid at this time.

If I have been badly injured, is there any compensation available?

Yes. You can sue for damages in law – for assault and battery, or for trespass. It is also possible to apply for compensation to the Criminal Injuries Compensation Board.

I'm too afraid of my partner, do I have to stay in my home?

An order may not be the answer for you. To find out more about your housing options, please see our leaflet *Do You Need a Safe Place to Stay?*

You cannot be forced to return home if you are too afraid. If you do wish to return, or stay in your own home with an order to protect you, talk to Women's Aid about your safety.

For example, do you need a phone to ring for help if your partner disobeys the order and approaches the house? Will your neighbours support you? What are your long-term plans?

Women's Aid can support you and offer practical suggestions.

What else should I know?

You are best protected by an order that has a power of arrest attached to it by the court. The power can only be given in certain defined circumstances.

Power of arrest means that, if the order is disobeyed, the police may arrest your violent partner – and they don't need a warrant.

Your partner should be brought before a judge or magistrates within 24 hours on a charge of 'contempt of court'. You may still be at risk unless he is held in custody. The penalty for contempt of court is a fine or imprisonment.

If the order has no power of arrest, and your partner disobeys it, he may be arrested for assault or breach of the peace if there is sufficient evidence. If not, you will need to ask your solicitor to take him back to court for breach of the order.

What is an undertaking?

Instead of making an order, some judges will ask you if you agree to accept an undertaking from your partner. An undertaking is a promise to the court. If it is instead of an order, this will probably be a promise not to hit or molest you.

The advantage of this is that you do not have to give evidence in court. The disadvantage is that an undertaking cannot have powers of arrest attached, so if the promise is broken, you and your solicitor need to go back to court.

In many areas, undertakings are treated less seriously and an undertaking is not the same or as good as an order.

In a case where you were hoping to get an order with a power of arrest attached (usually where you can prove physical injury), you can refuse to accept an undertaking and persist in asking for an order. It's best to discuss all this with your solicitor beforehand.

Violence against women violates their human rights

Mindful of violence

**Can violent men be 'cured' through therapy?
One man claims he was successfully treated. His wife says he
later tried to kill her. Emma Brooker listened to their stories**

At a recent Home Counties trial of a man charged with assaulting his partner, the court heard how the defendant had wrapped his girlfriend's baby in a sheet and used the child to batter her. His social worker told the court that she knew her client had difficulty controlling his temper and had tried to find him an anger management group. Unfortunately nothing was available at the time. She seemed to suggest that had a men's group been to hand, the attack might never have taken place.

But do therapy programmes for perpetrators of domestic violence really alter their behaviour? While men's therapy is seen by social services as a preventive measure, probation workers and magistrates are increasingly meting out therapy programmes for batterers as alternatives to prison sentences.

The Scottish Office funds two programmes which divert convicted batterers from custody; probation services nationwide run their own groups and schemes and London has four private or charity funded projects open to the public to which social services refer clients.

Berkshire Probation Service launched a therapy scheme in October. 'This is for men who have caused tremendous pain and hurt to their partners,' said John Roberts of BPS. 'Prison is likely – if anything – to increase men's violence, because it's a violent environment.'

Five years on from the founding of the first anger-management programmes in Britain many women's refuge and help-line workers are deeply sceptical about such projects which, they claim, may put battered women at even greater risk.

'Every few weeks, a woman contacts us whose partner is taking part in one of these men's therapy programmes,' says Kim Smith of London Women's Aid. 'Often he's using it as a leverage to get the woman to stay or come back. It's a form of emotional blackmail.' Julie Bindel of Justice For Women, a group which campaigns for change in the criminal justice system goes further. 'We know that men reoffend when perpetrator programmes are used as a substitute for punishment.

Women get a false sense of security and the men switch tactics. We have to look at misogyny rather than the acts of individual men whose mothers didn't love them.'

John Roberts of Berkshire Probation Service recognises the limitations of group therapy. 'Ideally we should be able to punish *and* get people on the programmes, but the resources are not available. We've involved the partners in our programme and as far as we know it has been successful,' he adds.

Here is the story of one man singled out as a success story by a London men's centre where he attended a therapy programme two hours a week for seven months on the recommendation of a psychiatrist. His wife contacted the *Guardian* a month later.

His story

I've never actually hit my wife with my fist. I've slapped and kicked her. On occasions when I've pushed her she's gone back and hit her head on the door or the wall. The marriage was good to begin with. Then I started drinking which caused arguments. I wasn't communicating with my wife. The truth is, I'd never really confided in anyone. This pattern of drinking and lashing out happened at least once a week. Other people thought it was acceptable, drinking people, bar people, people I worked with. They just said, wouldn't she shut up?

Well give her a slap, that type of attitude. My anger was just building up the whole time. To me it was totally acceptable.

I couldn't see that I was a woman beater. I always felt my wife was taking control of me somehow. Because I couldn't win an argument, I couldn't sit down and debate. I always used to feel that I was losing control. As a last resort I'd say I don't want to discuss that. By lashing out I was taking control of the situation.

After four years, my wife said that we would have to separate and that I would have to sort my life out. I needed to do something about my violence. When I first joined the men's group I said, 'I'm good with my hands and they said we know that Bill, that's why you're here.' It needed to be said. I had to face up to it – that I had been hitting my wife.

It was the first time somebody said to me that it is unacceptable to hit a woman, let alone your wife. They said stop it, it is wrong, there is help, there are alternatives. That was what I wanted to hear.

When I started going to the centre it was frightening. I didn't know what to expect. Every week we came in and the main topic was, have you hit your wife? I felt I was giving away all my life story and all my wife's bad points. They were picking up on things that I'd never thought about before, like my relationship with my father, who was a very closed, angry, violent man.

My violence didn't stop straight away. It made me focus on myself and question the build-up to my losing my temper. They told me to talk it out with my wife there and then. I started to say to her, 'Babe, I'm getting a resentment to this, or I feel bad about that,' and that was working.

I had quite a lot of respect for the other people in the group for being there. It became a priority for me to get to the men's group. I needed it and when I went there it made my wife feel more comfortable. I felt as if I'd conquered a major problem within myself by being able to open up and discuss how I was feeling. If I feel scared or insecure now, which is only human, I stand up and say it whereas before I couldn't.

We both want to get back together but I won't give my flat up until I know what I learnt in the men's group is sitting comfortably with me. My wife totally agrees.

Her story

Bill treated me like a princess when we first met. If someone swore in front of me he'd say, this lady is not used to this sort of behaviour, please do not swear in her company, I thought, what a gentleman, what a charmer.

We got married and he moved into my flat in 1988. About three months after he'd moved in, I contradicted him in front of a friend. He took me upstairs and whacked me in the face, my lip swelled right up.

It just got worse. We went to the pub one night. He bought me a rose and treated me nice but he told me to sit in the corner. I couldn't talk to my friends. When Bill walked out the door, I followed and he said, 'where the hell do you think you're going?' He head-butted me. He took the rose and whacked me with it. He brought me back to the house, took my keys, locked me in and said, 'stay in you bitch.' At first it didn't occur to me to leave. I couldn't believe what was happening. One particular day I was covered in bruises because he kicked and punched me. He looked at me and started crying and said, 'I'm sorry. I don't know what's the matter with me. It's best if you just keep quiet when I'm in that mood.'

One night in 1992 he was very drunk. I was outside talking to the neighbour and he dragged me into the kitchen, put his fingers down my throat, took a large knife out and tried to cut my tongue out. He said, 'I'm going to do it this time, I'm going to kill you.' I ended up in accident and emergency in hospital.

After that, I asked Bill to leave. He promised he would get help and started being very nice. That lasted a few months, but one night he got drunk and accused me of going out in a short skirt. He started to strangle me. I went unconscious and when I came round, he was sitting watching the television.

I couldn't take any more. I started planning to kill him. I thought that's the only way I can get this man out of my life. He would be dead but I would be safer. I was too scared to leave.

Around that time he grabbed me and smashed my head against the wall. I got out the house, ran to the phone box and dialled 999. An ambulance took me to hospital. The police turned up and Bill had barricaded himself into the house. He gave himself up the next day and was charged with assault and criminal damage because he'd smashed up some furniture. He was fined £500 for the damage and was bound over to keep the peace. But he wasn't convicted for GBH, he was just cautioned. I thought he'd be put away.

I got an injunction to get him out of my flat and the council put him in a bedsit. When I began divorce proceedings, he started going to the men's centre for counselling. I thought, wonderful, the violence will stop. We met now and again and he didn't hit me during that time. When he finished the programme he said,

it's worked. I'll never ever hit you again and I believed him.

The last time I saw him he raped me. I had decided to go ahead with the divorce and told him so. He followed me one night and pulled me into the passage of his place, turned the lights off and said, 'I know you're going to divorce me, I don't care if I go to prison. I'm going to have you one last time.'

I thought I was going to die. My shoe got broken, my tights were ripped as he tried to penetrate me. I kept crying and screaming. He put something across my mouth. I kept choking. I couldn't breathe. When he got off and put the light on he said, 'don't go out there like that, you'll get me nicked.' I looked a wreck. He give me five pounds to get a cab. When I got home I dialled the police. They sent two officers, but I didn't want to be examined.

When I told them Bill's family lived across the road, they said they understood. My solicitor got an injunction. Social services have just had the iron gate put up over the front door. I didn't press charges. I just couldn't do it. He would have killed me. He said that going to the men's group would help him if he ever got into trouble. He might have used that in court. I'm planning to move away now. I'm thinking of changing my name.

Names have been changed.

Domestic violence – you can face up to it

Do you assault your partner?

Assaulting your partner is a crime and is as serious as assaulting anyone else.

There can be no justification for violence. You cannot blame it on pressure of work, you cannot blame it on drink, you cannot blame it on financial worries or anything else. Most of all, you cannot blame it on your partner, no matter what the circumstances.

Your violent behaviour towards your partner is no one's responsibility but yours. There can be no excuses. Only you can stop – and you can stop.

Take action now

If you think that a situation may arise at some time in the future when you might become violent towards your partner, you can take action now to reduce the risks. Taking these simple steps can help:

Think about when you have been violent in the past. What were the circumstances? Try to anticipate such situations in the future and avoid them if you can.

Agree with your partner in advance that, should a potentially violent situation arise, you will 'walk away' – leave the house – for a fixed period of one hour. This will give you time to calm down. If after that time you have still not calmed down, phone your partner if you can, and say that you will stay away for another hour. Continue to do this until you feel composed enough to return home and your partner agrees that it is alright.

It is difficult to think straight as you become angrier. Therefore you should agree with your partner beforehand where you will go to calm down.

There are lots of options, but never take drink or drugs – these will not help.

And don't keep going over the argument in your head – this will only make matters worse. It will also mean that you take longer to calm down.

Finding help

If you find that you are unable to stop assaulting your partner, there are people who can help you.

General Practitioner
Your GP may be able to assist and can, if considered appropriate, refer you for specialist help.

Social Work Department
Your local Social Work Department can also provide advice and guidance about what steps

you should take. Their number is listed in your local telephone directory under your Region or Islands Council or can be obtained from Directory Enquiries by dialling 192.

Marriage Counselling Services
While responsibility for assaulting your partner is yours and yours alone, counselling may be able to help you through your situation. A number of local marriage counselling services are available throughout Scotland. Whether or not you are married, a counsellor is available to assist. Counselling is completely confidential and all counsellors are highly trained and experienced in helping people like you. You may attend either on your own or with your partner.

© The Scottish Office
June, 1995

Teenager in the refuge

This article is for you to read if you are a teenager who has come to stay with your mother in a Women's Aid Refuge

Coming into a refuge . . .

A refuge is a safe house where women and children can come to live for a while when things have been bad at home.

There are refuges all over Wales, and elsewhere in the UK, so that women and children can get away from violence and trouble.

The refuge you have come to may be an ordinary house, or one that has been specially adapted. More than one family lives in it at a time.

You'll have a bedroom with the rest of your family and share the living room, kitchen and bathroom with the other families. Your mother will still look after you, like she did when you were at home.

There are women who come into the refuge now and then, but don't live there, called workers. If you need to know anything, or if something is bothering you, they might be able to help.

All refuges have some rules. They are not there to boss you about, just to keep everyone safe. Ask a worker or your mother about them if you haven't seen them.

School . . .

You go to school as normal from the refuge. If you have to change schools, you'll get help to sort out things like school uniform and transport.

You may feel you don't want to tell friends you're in a refuge. You can say your staying with another family for a while. Teachers will know you're in a refuge, but you don't have to tell anyone else.

Staying in the refuge . . .

Living in a house with people you don't know and kids of all ages running around may seem hard, but everyone in the refuge is in the same boat, and it is great when everyone mucks in and helps each other.

Sometimes the place or the people in it will get on your nerves. When this happens, it can help to go out for a while, even if it's just for a walk or to see a friend. Ask a worker for some local information about buses, leisure centres, youth clubs, etc.

Photo: Julian Nieman

Otherwise, you could go to your family's bedroom and try to be on your own for a while. Everyone needs a bit of peace sometimes and the younger kids can get quite high in the refuge, especially when they first come in.

It's a good idea to keep your belongings in your family's room, to keep them safe from the younger children.

Remember that they are feeling mixed up too, and try to be as patient as you can with them.

The refuge works best when everyone is trying to make the best of things.

If you have any ideas or suggestions that might be useful, let everyone know. And if you can help by showing a new family round, moving furniture or taking younger kids out for instance, you'll find that sometimes giving help makes you feel better.

Also, if things seem awful at times, remember that your stay in the refuge is not for keeps – you will be moving on and then you can come back to visit if you want – you might find that you miss the place for a while, even if you can't wait to leave!

Your mother and you . . .

When you first come in, everything you've known will seem to be lost. You may miss your father, your home, your mates or the road you live in.

But don't assume that it's all gone for good – things will get better, you'll get used to the changes and start enjoying yourself again.

You may feel annoyed at your mother. Remember she wouldn't have left your Dad, home and everything else easily, and she must be feeling pretty bad about things too.

You and her may not have the same feelings about what's happened. That's OK – there's no rule that says that you have to feel the same, but it helps if you try and see things from her point of view, and if she does the same for you.

It might help to sit down and talk about it, or if that's not possible ask a worker to help out.

Sometimes it helps to have someone who's not involved to talk to, and remember – everything may seem upside down at the moment, but things will get sorted out.

© Welsh Women's Aid

35

Domestic violence – don't stand for it

Domestic violence is a serious crime. Nobody has the right to abuse you physically, sexually or emotionally. Everyone has the right to live their life free of violence, fear and abuse.

If you are in a violent relationship, remember that you are not alone. There are people who can help you.

You may feel frightened, humiliated, alone, ashamed and confused. You are not to blame – if a man assaults his wife or girlfriend, whatever the reason, he is the one with a problem and should recognise it.

There is still a lot of confusion and misunderstanding about domestic violence – what it is, who suffers from it, who commits it and why.

Violence or abuse suffered by women in their home which is carried out by their partner, ex-partner or anyone they are living with is known as domestic violence. Victims of domestic violence are usually women, but this is not always the case.

Women experience domestic violence regardless of their social group, class, age, race, disability, sexuality and lifestyle – it knows no boundaries. Violence and abuse can begin at any time – in the first year or after years of marriage or living together.

Domestic violence can take a number of forms such as physical assault, sexual abuse, rape, and threats. In addition, it may include mental and verbal abuse and humiliation. Your partner may not give you any money, constantly criticise you or forbid you to see your friends and family. He may be caring one day and violent the next. He may offer 'rewards' on certain conditions, or in an attempt to persuade you that the abuse won't happen again. However persuasive he may seem, it is likely to get worse over time.

It is not easy to accept that someone you love and have trusted can behave so aggressively towards you. Because they can't explain their partner's behaviour, many women assume that they are to blame.

You have the right to be free of fear and abuse. It is your partner whose behaviour needs to change.

Women experiencing domestic violence tend to play down rather than exaggerate the violence. For some the decision to seek help, to leave the abuser, or get the abuser to leave, is quickly and easily made. For many, the decision will be long and painful as they try to make the relationship work and stop the violence.

Only you can judge your own situation. The groups at the end of this booklet can offer you help and advice and talk through the various options that are available to you. Women who leave often return to their partners hoping for an improvement in the relationship or because of financial/social pressures. Never be afraid to ask for help again. Some women may leave many times before making their final decision.

You should seek legal advice from your local Women's Aid Group, Law Centre, Citizens' Advice Bureau or a solicitor if you are concerned about your children. They can advise you on issues such as parental responsibility, where children should live, with whom they should have contact, changes of school and other related problems.

Despite what their partners say, women do have legal rights in relation to their children. Some men say that, if their partner leaves or tells anybody about the violence, their children will be taken away from them. In most cases this will not happen.

Children will react in different ways to being brought up in a home with a violent person.

They may be affected by the tension or by witnessing arguments and assaults. They may feel that they are to blame, or feel insecure, alone, frightened or confused – like you.

Talk to them. Be honest with them about the situation they are in. They need to know that the violence is not their fault and that they are not responsible for the way their father/your partner behaves. They should be told that violence is wrong and does not solve problems.

Men who are abusive to women do not necessarily abuse children, but it can happen. If you suspect that this has happened, it is important to talk to them about it and to take steps to protect them (e.g. by seeking advice from Social Services). Social workers will not take your children away if they can work with you to make sure they are safe.

If you are experiencing violence and abuse in the home, there are three steps you can take:

- the first step is to recognise that it is happening to you and to stop playing down the abuse you are experiencing
- the second step is to recognise that you are not to blame. No one deserves to be assaulted, humiliated or abused, least of all by their partner in a supposedly caring relationship – there is no excuse
- the third step is to begin seeking the help and support that is available.

Where to go for support and advice if you are in a violent relationship

If you are being abused by someone, there are organisations that can give you practical and emotional support.

Refuges
Refuges provide safe emergency and temporary accommodation, advice, information, support and a range of

other services for women and children escaping violence.

Women's Aid is a key support agency for women and children experiencing domestic violence. The organisation is run by women for women. Women's Aid England runs a domestic violence helpline for women experiencing violence and abuse in the home. If you need to talk to someone – perhaps for the first time – about the situation you are in, they can offer a sympathetic ear and clear information about housing, legal and other rights.

Their services are confidential and completely free.

Look in the telephone directory for the telephone number of your local Women's Aid group or local refuge. Social Services, the Samaritans, Housing Departments and police stations can also give you your Women's Aid local number. Most groups are on call 24 hours a day.

The Samaritans
The Samaritans offer confidential emotional support 24 hours a day by phone, face-to-face or by letter. There are over 200 branches in the UK and Eire staffed by trained volunteers. See your telephone directory for local numbers and addresses or ask the operator who will put you through directly.

The police
Domestic violence is a crime which the police now deal with as a very serious matter.

They will be sympathetic and offer practical help and advice. Most forces have specially trained and experienced officers who will listen and speak to you separately from your partner.

You can ask to be seen by a woman officer and, if you wish, they can arrange medical aid, transport and a safe place for you to go.

Their first priority is your safety and well-being.

How do I contact the police?
In an emergency dial 999.

Otherwise, you can contact your local police station. They can put you in touch with trained officers who will let you know what other help is available and will offer you support.

Victim Support
Offers information and support to victims of crime. There is a special leaflet for women who have been sexually assaulted, and a support service provided by trained volunteers. All help given is free and confidential. You can contact Victim Support direct, or ask the police to put you in contact with your local group.

Health
Many women don't realise the impact their partner's behaviour can have on their health.

They may experience depression and anxiety problems which are often just as severe as any physical ones. This may happen after they have left the relationship because of all the changes and upheavals.

Try to talk about your feelings rather than block them out. If you have to go to casualty, try and be open about the cause of your injuries. You can do this in complete confidence.

Talk to your GP or Health Visitor. Tell them the real cause of your worries and injuries. This is vital if they are to give you the proper medical help and support that you need.

Find out if there is a local support group you could go to which could offer you help and counselling.

Your local Social Services Department may also be able to offer you support, particularly if you or your children need care.

Whatever you decide, don't suffer alone. There are lots of people who can help. And don't feel ashamed of what has happened to you – it is not your fault.

Domestic violence is a serious crime. Nobody has the right to abuse you physically, sexually or emotionally. Everyone has the right to live their life free of violence, fear and abuse

---

Money
One of the reasons that many women stay in an abusive relationship is because they wonder how they will manage financially if they leave.

There are various benefits which you may be able to claim and some can be paid even if you are working. Your local Social Security Benefits Agency Office will be able to advise you which benefits you can claim. General advice about social security benefits can be obtained by calling Freeline Social Security on 0800 666 555.

Housing
Many women stay in a violent relationship because they fear there is nowhere else to go.

There are several options open to you.

If you have had to leave your home because of violence, you will not be seen as deliberately making yourself homeless and the Council may have a legal duty to help you. It will look into your case and, if it concludes that it has a duty to assist you, will provide temporary accommodation at once and a longer-term home when something suitable becomes available.

For more information contact your Local Housing Office.

Other options range from staying with family or friends or going to a women's refuge, through to renting or buying new accommodation or gaining control of your own home.

Remember
- Domestic violence is a serious crime.
- Everyone has the right to live their life free of fear, threats and abuse.
- If you are a victim you are not alone – there are people who can help you.
- Your partner's violence is not your fault.

Contact Women's Aid and/or the Police for further help and advice.

You can contact the Women's Aid England helpline on 0117 963 3542

In Wales you can call Welsh Women's Aid on 01222 390874 in office hours.

© Home Office Relations Branch

INDEX

ADDITIONAL RESOURCES

You might like to contact the following organisations for further information. Due to the increasing cost of postage, many organisations cannot respond to inquiries unless they receive a stamped, addressed envelope.

Childline
2nd Floor Royal Mail Building
Studd Street
London
N1 0QW
Tel: 0171 239 1000
Fax: 0171 239 1001

Citizens Advice Bureau
Free information on money, housing, legal rights, local groups. Look in the phone book under Citizens.

National Alliance of Women's Organisations
279-281 Whitechapel Road
London
E1 1BY
Tel: 0171 381 3916

To eliminate all forms of discrimination. Policy work on issues of importance to women ie. representation in the media, rural issues, black and ethnic minorities and education etc.

National Council of Women of Great Britain
36 Danbury Street
London
N1 8JU
Tel: 0171 354 2395
Fax: 0171 354 9214

Against all discrimination against women.

National Society for the Prevention of Cruelty to Children (NSPCC)
National Centre
42 Curtain Road
London
EC2A 3NH
Tel: 0171 825 2500

National Youth Agency
17-23 Albion Street
Leicester
LE1 6GD
Tel: 0116 2856789
Fax: 0116 2471043

NCH Action for Children
85 Highbury Park
London
N5 1UD
Tel: 0171 226 2033
Fax: 0171 226 2537

Runs family and community centres nationwide for children and families who are victims of domestic violence.

Newham Asian Women's Project
PO Box 225
London
E7 9AA
Tel: 0181 472 0528
Fax: 0181 503 5673

Provides an Asian perspective on violence in the home.

Northern Ireland Women's Aid
129 University Street
Belfast
BT7 1HP
Tel: 01232 249 041

Police Federation of England and Wales
Croonin House
245 Church Street
London
N9 9HW
Tel: 0181 803 0255
Fax: 0181 803 1761

Refuge
PO Box 855
London
W4 4JF
Tel: 0181 747 0133
Fax: 0181 994 9592

Has a student information pack available for £3:00. Information on domestic violence.

24 hour crisis line: Tel: 0181 995 4430

Save the Children
17 Grove Lane
London

SE5 8RD
Tel: 0171 703 5400
Fax: 0171 703 2278

Produces a wide range of materials. Ask for their catalogue.

The Children's Society
Edward Rudolf House
Margery Street
London
WC1X 0JL
Tel: 0171 837 4299

Scottish Women's Aid
12 Torphichen St
Edinburgh
EH3 8JQ
Tel: 0131 221 0401

Victim Support
Cranmer House
39 Brixton Road
London
SW9 6DZ
Tel: 0171 735 9166

Has range of leaflets on various types of support offered by Victim Support.

Welsh Women's Aid
38-48 Crwys Road
Cardiff
CF2 4NNO
Tel: 01222 390874

Women Against Rape (WAR)
King's Cross Women's Centre
71 Tonbridge Street
London
WC1H 9DZ
Tel: 0171 837 7509
Fax: 0171 833 4817

Third world/black women aiming to dismantle racism, sexism, poverty etc

Women's Aid Federation England
PO Box 391
Bristol
BS99 7WS
Tel: 0117 9633 494

ACKNOWLEDGEMENTS

The publisher is grateful for permission to reproduce the following material

Chapter One: Domestic Violence

What is domestic violence?, © BBC Radio Two, June 1995, *Victims of crime*, © British Crime Survey (BCS), 1995, *The extent of the problem*, © HMSO Reproduced with the kind permission of Her Majesty's Stationery Office, October 1994, *Abused women*, © Scottish Women's Aid, *If you are an abused woman*, © Refuge, 1994, *'So why don't they leave?'*, © Newham Asian Women's Project, 1995, *The legal options*, © Northern Ireland Women's Aid Federation, June 1995, *Different kinds of abuse*, BBC Radio Two, June 1995, *The fear of going home*, © The Telegraph Plc, London 1995, *Michael Howard announces new circular to combat domestic violence*, © HMSO Reproduced with the Kind Permission of Her Majesty's Stationery Office, *Government's campaign offers victims little help*, © Women Against Rape Britain, October 1994, *Violence against women*, © Women's National Commission, 1994, *The hidden victims*, © NCH Action for Children, 1994, *Children's experiences of living with domestic violence*, © Children's Legal Centre, *Violence in the home leaves children in need*, © Community Care, April 1995, *The problems facing black, Asian and ethnic minority women*, BBC Radio Two, June 1995, *Key principles*, © Refuge, *Why I had to find Beth and Mandy guilty*, © The Guardian, May 1995, *Battered men come out of the closet*, © The Independent, April 1995, *Battered husbands afraid to seek help*, © The Sunday Telegraph Plc, London 1995, *The battered male?*, © The Irish Times, February 1995.

Chapter Two: Seeking help

Running from pain, © Community Care, February/March 1995, *Some of the myths of women abuse*, © Refuge, March 1995, *What can a woman expect from Women's Aid?*, © Scottish Women's Aid, March 1995, *Domestic violence and medical services*, © Northern Ireland Women's Aid Federation, June 1995, *Do you need legal protection against violence*, © Welsh Women's Aid, *Mindful of violence*, © The Guardian, April 1995, *Domestic violence – you can face up to it*, © The Scottish Office, *Teenager in the refuge*, © Welsh Women's Aid, *Domestic violence – don't stand for it*, © HMSO Reproduced with the kind Permission of Her Majesty's Stationery Office.

Photographs and Illustrations

Pages 1, 16, 25: Emma Dodd/Folio Collective, pages 3, 12, 34: Anthony Haythornthwaite/Folio Collective, page 4: Scottish Women's Aid, pages 9, 22: Andrew Smith/Folio Collective, page 18: Maggie Murray/Format, page 31: Suzanne Roden/Format, page 35: Julian Nieman.

Craig Donnellan
Cambridge
September, 1995